Praise for *Live Your Happy*

"As a writer and reader who has lived with dyslexia just like Maria Felipe, I always appreciate a short book that gets right to the point, then sticks to it. Maria's point is that happiness is an inside job. While getting out of the habit of unhappiness requires some work, it's well worth it. And Maria does a great job of reminding us that getting happier should be fun!"

— **Gerald G. Jampolsky, MD**, author of
Love Is Letting Go of Fear

"Maria Felipe's book, *Live Your Happy*, is as simple as it is challenging. She leads you by the hand gently, with motherly love, and at the same time releases you out into the world with her insightful guidance and easy-to-do exercises that will surely transform your life and allow you to find your happy. I have read a lot of self-help books in my life, but I've never found one so simple, clear, authentic, and relatable in its message. Maria takes the self-help genre to another level where she bluntly lets you know that reading this book will not make you happy. That, to me, is simply brilliant and refreshing!"

— **Eva Tamargo**, actress,
Passions and *The Haves and the Have Nots*

"*Live Your Happy* is a brief and lively guide to overcoming fear, living authentically, and finding inner happiness regardless of outer circumstances. Reading Maria Felipe's crisp, down-to-earth prose is less like reading a self-help book and more like having a conversation with a trusted friend."

— **Marci Shimoff**, *New York Times*–bestselling author of
Happy for No Reason

"Having known Maria Felipe for many years and having heard her speak her truth, I knew this would be an excellent book. I wasn't disappointed. I believe *Live Your Happy* will make you more aware of your true nature and help you live your life in a way that will remove the barriers that prevent you from experiencing it. I highly recommend this important and entertaining book."

— **Gary Renard**, bestselling author of
The Disappearance of the Universe trilogy

"The best thing about *Live Your Happy* is the practical examples that Maria Felipe shares about putting the ideas from *A Course in Miracles* into practice. Happiness is our natural essence, and Maria shows this in her transparency and her willingness to trust in Spirit."

— **David Hoffmeister**, author of
Quantum Forgiveness: Physics, Meet Jesus

LIVE YOUR
HAPPY

LIVE YOUR
HAPPY

GET OUT OF YOUR OWN WAY AND
FIND THE LOVE WITHIN

Maria Felipe

New World Library
Novato, California

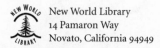

New World Library
14 Pamaron Way
Novato, California 94949

Text design by Megan Colman

Library of Congress Cataloging-in-Publication data is available.

First printing, April 2017
Print ISBN 978-1-60868-453-3
Ebook ISBN 978-1-60868-454-0

Printed in the United States on 100% postconsumer-waste recycled paper

10   9   8   7   6   5   4   3   2   1

I happily dedicate this book to *mi mami* (my mom) — no matter my learning disabilities, she always made me feel as if I was the smartest and most talented girl in the world.

Contents

Foreword

When you meet Maria Felipe, you're immediately aware that you're dealing with a woman who is confident, cheerful, honest, forthright, and happy. We met not long ago, during the early stages of a TV project that would have been a dream come true for both of us. Although the project was never produced, what I got from the experience was my acquaintance with the other great women involved, and I can say without a doubt that Maria was foremost among them.

From the moment we met, I could see in Maria a friend, and I was not mistaken. We started chatting, and between laughs, she mentioned that she was a minister in a church. *What?!* This was a big surprise and a lesson; I had always thought that women dedicated to spirituality wouldn't look as pretty and put-together as Maria — but then, being out of the ordinary is a part of who she is! So there I was, in front of this woman who instead of giving me a "sermon" made me laugh and seemed to help me connect some "loose wiring" in my head. I immediately formed a strong bond with her. We continued chatting, and I discovered that she is a teacher of *A Course in Miracles*, a book that saved my life. Suddenly everything made sense. I understood how someone who had gone through so many trials in life could be there in front of me, whole, laughing, ready to live, to soar, to enjoy, and above all to always be happy.

Reading *Live Your Happy* was very similar to my first encounter with Maria. It gives you a glimpse into a reality that seems too good to be true — authentic, safe, and always happy. From the first paragraph, it's easy to let yourself be carried by the words. Bit by bit, without realizing it, you remember old mistakes that were dormant but still hurt, and you realize what you must still get over, forgive, accept, and be thankful for. As you continue, you get to know the true Maria as she recounts the tough moments she had to go through in order to live in happiness. It is then that you come to understand more, to know her a bit better, to see your own struggles in hers, and to feel the desire for spiritual growth and happiness even more. And at the end of every chapter are the ingredients and steps for this particular recipe — mantras, prayers, and all the tools needed to reach the goal: "live your happy."

Ever since I found *A Course in Miracles,* I have tried to find the best way to help friends and family who cry out for help (sometimes unconsciously), but it's no easy task to help them understand. Look, I know better than anyone the work it takes. But once we get our mind in order and start working with the right tools, it's not as hard as it seems. The problem is getting to that point: leaving the ego behind and realizing that we need to change, that we deserve to be happy, and that we must give ourselves permission to do so. Living in darkness so often renders us blind, and fear does everything it can to keep us from regaining our sight. But once we find the light switch, once we know that the curtains had been drawn the whole time, curiosity alone is enough to make us want to turn on the lights or to open the curtains and let sunlight into our lives.

Once I read *Live Your Happy*, it not only confirmed how talented, friendly, and wise Maria is, but also reminded me of the places I should never return to, of the mistakes that have become a habit. It gave me the encouragement to overcome them one day at a time and provided me with the steps I need to follow in those tough moments when life doesn't go according to plan. Everything depends on how we react and on whether we want to learn from those trials or not.

In *Live Your Happy*, you will find the easiest way to deal with the ego, with fear, and with all those false ideas that were fed into our minds and that can turn into little hells that slowly consume us. In this book Maria shows you the easiest way to find the light switch — to stop living in darkness and to be reborn in the light, where all of us should be.

Maria is a woman who has learned from all the lessons life has given her and, instead of staying stuck in regret, continues to move forward. Best of all, she tells us how she did it and how we, too, can move ahead, smiling at life. The most wonderful part is that *Live Your Happy* gives us the recipe to simply be happy. And, the book being exactly like Maria, it does so in a fun, direct, honest way. It also lets us read about all the experiences that made Maria the great woman she now is. The most beautiful thing about my friend is that she doesn't want happiness just for herself; her mission in this life is to spread the word, to spread the message that happiness does indeed exist, that it is in our hands and — can you believe it? — it is not as difficult to attain as it seems.

Thank you, Maria, for teaching us how to "live our happy."

— Angélica Vale, acclaimed Mexican actress,
singer, and comedian

Introduction

Here is the truth about you: You're strong, you're powerful, you're *enough* — and you are not alone.

In fact, that's true for each one of us. But if that's so, why don't we feel this way all the time? Why do we still have ups and downs, feeling really good one day and crying our eyes out the next? Why do we read dozens, if not hundreds, of self-help books and attend numerous seminars, and yet still feel unhappy and unfulfilled? We try one job after another, one romance after another, even one religion after another, and yet we still often don't know our life's purpose — or why our "happy" often feels so far away.

I've been there and felt the same, and what I've learned about real happiness is the reason this book has come to life. You can repeat affirmations all day long, or walk on hot coals, but you will not *live your happy* until you understand the way your mind works and recognize your own divinity. I am not saying this lightly, and I am not saying that getting there will be easy. But you can do it — and if you're reading this book, the time has come to get started.

We're in this together. As you wake up to your truth, I wake up to mine. I will share with you spiritual tools that really work, but you must put them to use. If you do, you will be helping everyone live the happiness they deserve.

Where I'm Coming From

Before I became a minister and teacher of *A Course in Miracles*, I was an actress, a model, and a TV host. I was in magazines, runway shows, TV shows, and national commercials. I was the first Latina boxing announcer. I can still hear myself announcing: "In the red corner, from Los Mochis, Mexico, weighing 139½ pounds, Humberto Soto! And in the blue corner, from Guadalajara, Mexico, weighing 140 pounds, Jorge Solís!" Later, working for the world-famous WWF (now the WWE, or World Wrestling Entertainment), I interviewed competitors live in front of an audience of twenty thousand people. That might sound really exciting. In fact, it was horrifying.

I remember walking down the ramp toward the ring feeling so scared; my heart pounded like it was going to come out of my chest. All I could think was: *Can I do this? Am I good enough? Will the people like me? Will I get the contract to host the rest of the shows?*

At least I had an amazingly romantic French boyfriend. He was a sweetheart and very thoughtful. When I was featured in *People en Español*, he bought all the copies he could find, and he surprised me with them at the airport when I came home. Yet no matter what this guy did, I always felt unworthy of his love, and I was fixated on the worry that he would cheat on me.

I had a great career, a wonderful boyfriend, a nice apartment near the beach in Miami...and I was *miserable*. I was reading all the self-help books I could lay my hands on, going to workshops, and declaring affirmations, and none of it made me happy.

In other words, I was a hot mess back in the day. I did not know any better, but now I know that we always do the best we can with the awareness we have at that moment. When I was in my twenties, I longed to be loved — loved by everyone, loved by the whole world. What I didn't know was that I was really searching for the love of God...and that I already had that love within me!

I could not bring happiness into my experience because I was in a trance, living like a puppet run by my own ego. It was ego that told me I'd be happy when I booked that commercial, won that Oscar, or got married and had kids. All my unsolvable problems determined my reality, and every problem was a *big deal*. The harder I looked for love, the farther away from me it seemed to be.

In 1995 I came across Marianne Williamson's book *A Return to Love*. At that time I was going through a major depression, and her words were very comforting. But what affected me most were the quotes from another book called

A Course in Miracles. I had never heard of that strange blue book before, and it would be six years before I actually began to study it. While browsing the bookstore of the Unity on the Bay Church in Miami, I heard an announcement that an introductory class on *A Course in Miracles* was beginning in the next room. I was intrigued, so I went. I wasn't quite prepared for what the teacher said: We are wholly responsible for our experiences; we are not victims of anyone or anything; only love is real and all else is an illusion.

I'll admit that I was shocked. *I am responsible for everything I see, and I am not a victim of the world?* I just wasn't ready to buy that. The teacher went on to say that the Course focused on true forgiveness, which he defined as the understanding that no one has really done *anything* to you. *¿Qué, qué?*

That's when I fell out of my chair...and I mean literally. It was very embarrassing to pick myself up in front of everyone! Yet as I did so, I had the powerful sensation that I had found my path, even though I really didn't understand anything of what the teacher was saying at the time.

Twenty years after first reading about *A Course in Miracles* (*ACIM*) — and after much study to acquire my ministerial certificate from the *ACIM* school known as Pathways of Light — I'm a little clearer on the message. This self-study spiritual thought system helps students develop a relationship with the "internal teacher" it calls the Holy Spirit, which in turn helps us change how we see the world on a daily basis. This "shift in perception" is what *ACIM* calls a *miracle.*

How to Use This Book

For me, *A Course in Miracles* provides the inner tools to become free of bondage to the sickness of the ego, so that we can finally discover all the power within us. The Course puts it this way: "Your task is not to seek for love, but merely to seek and find all the barriers within yourself that you have built against it" (*ACIM*, ch. 6, section IV).

Let's be clear: Seeking and finding all the barriers we've built against love is *not fun*. We have to face feelings of sadness, abandonment, fear, and loss and take responsibility for them all. We have to learn to trust the voice of our inner teacher instead of our own worst advice, which basically means getting over ourselves. We have to stop trying to manipulate people, stop trying to make things happen the way we want them to happen, and most importantly, stop looking for happiness "out there" where it will never be found.

This book is a simple but not necessarily easy guide to learning to *live your happy*. I will share practical spiritual tools to get you there, along with stories of my own journey and of people I've counseled. I empower my clients not by telling them what to do but by helping them understand that they have the answer *within*.

That being said, I ask that you trust me and be gentle with yourself. Step by step, I will train you to listen to your right mind. In turn, you will become free to live in happiness consistently. You will even be happy when you have so-called problems. How's that for a miracle?

Setting an Intention

In the same way that I begin all my workshops, I offer this book with an intention. An intention is different than an *expectation*, which ultimately makes us unhappy. For instance, I advise you not to expect this book to *make you happy*. There is nothing outside yourself that can give you your happy, including this book. My intention is for this book to help you see that you have all the happiness you could ever want already — waiting to be recognized within. As the Course puts it: "If you will lay aside the ego's voice, however loudly it may seem to call; if you will not accept its petty gifts that give you nothing that you really want; if you listen with an open mind, that has not told you what salvation is; then you will hear the mighty voice of truth, quiet in power, strong in stillness, and completely certain in its messages" (*ACIM*, workbook lesson 106).

The secret of *living your happy* is that you don't have to find something or someone that's missing before you can claim it. But it is useful to identify any barriers that get in the way of *living your happy* — including fear, impatience, and doubt. We'll look more closely at those barriers as we go along. For now, just be willing to give up whatever might be blocking your well-deserved joy. This is how you will get out of your own way and let the will of God — which is the same as *the intention of love* — be accomplished instead.

I will be your spiritual coach, but *you* will need to do the work. Right now all you need is what the Course calls "a little willingness," and the rest will follow. Declare now: *I am willing*. And then let's do this!

Dearest Holy Spirit,

I hand over my experience of this book to you. I am willing to let go of my expectations and simply enjoy the ride. I allow you to come into my mind, opening the door for me to see whatever needs to be seen, so I may heal and live the happiness I am worthy of. Guide me on what to read or reread, how much time to spend on this reading, and how I can apply the teachings that will work best for me.

Amen

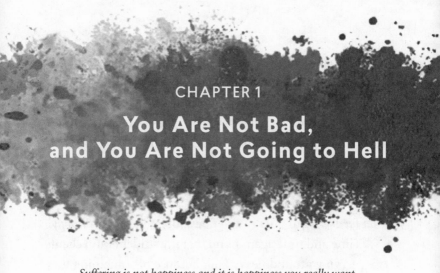

CHAPTER 1

You Are Not Bad, and You Are Not Going to Hell

Suffering is not happiness and it is happiness you really want.

— *ACIM*, workbook lesson 73

People often suffer from trying to live up to expectations that have been imposed on them. These expectations may come from a church, a community, or even one's own family. When I was eighteen, I attended a Catholic retreat where I was expected to confess my sins to a priest. Yikes! I remember thinking that this couldn't be right because:

1. I was not a sinner, and
2. if I was, why would I confess to a total stranger?!

I also attended a lecture where I was told that one shouldn't have sex before marriage and that liking someone of the same sex was wrong. I was laughing inside, thinking, *This is just stupid!*

My parents are of different religions. My dad is Presbyterian, and my mom is Catholic. When I told them I was not comfortable with what I heard at church, they told me I could choose my religion when I was older. That was a true blessing because they recognized that, even though I was young, I knew the truth. We all know the truth; we just forget it sometimes. What gets in the way of remembering the truth within is usually guilt — a parasite in our minds that feeds on our energy and does not let us *live our happy*!

Time and time again I find that my students and clients are carrying around heavy guilt because of something they did in the past, leading them to believe that they are basically bad. They say things like:

"I lied and cheated, and then I left my family."

"I 'came out' to my parents and family too early."

"Because I did something really bad in the past,
      I am no longer like everyone else."

A Course in Miracles suggests instead that we all feel guilty for just one reason: We think we have separated from God. Even if we seem to have many problems, this is really the only problem. This might be hard to understand at first; I didn't get it for a while, either. For now, I just ask you to trust me about this, and I'll help you understand it as we go along.

Who Is God?

First of all, who is God really? The Course sums it up very simply: "God is but love, and therefore so am I." What this means is that our Source is pure love, not some punishing Father who wants us to confess our sins, follow commandments, and believe only certain things and not others. For a lot of us, love can often seem to be very far away. Without really thinking it through, we tend to blame ourselves for our distance from love.

Once we believe we have separated from God, our Source of love, as if that weren't punishment enough, then we begin to fear being punished for turning away. Because we believe we *should* be punished, we do it to ourselves. We start creating unsolvable problems — what I call our "big deals" — so we can pay for the mistake of separating from God. Then we get obsessed with our big deals instead of the real problem underneath them all. As the Course suggests, *we are never upset for the reason we think.*

Before you know it, we've created an entire world of illusions where we think we can hide from a cruel God — who never wanted to punish us in the first place. We're followed everywhere by our self-created guilt. That doesn't feel too good, so then we decide all our problems are somebody else's fault.

That means we project our guilt onto the world, and now we are really screwed. The result of our projections is distrust, unhappiness, and betrayal between individuals and even war between cultures and nations. We suspect others of causing our misery, and we get locked into conflicts, big and small, that we just can't seem to resolve. We usually don't see that our conflicts are rooted in the belief that we somehow turned away from God and lost touch with love.

How Did We Lose Touch with Love?

In the beginning, there was perfect happiness. Sometimes this state is referred to metaphorically as the Garden of Eden, but it's really a state of mind that's pure bliss. Ecstasy! No judgments, sadness, anger, or sickness existed…only *love*. Then arose a very silly thought: "Is there something else?" That was the beginning of doubt, and as the Course suggests, "No one has been sure of anything since" (*ACIM*, ch. 3, section V).

Exactly when did this mistaken thought occur? The answer is: just a moment ago.

It's happened countless times before, but the only time that counts is the most recent one because the only time that matters is *now*. We are constantly thinking that we are separate from God, removing ourselves from the love that is our true nature. That's why we remain in such a painful world. How long we've been there is really beside the point.

If you want to *live your happy* instead of being trapped in a world of separation, you have to understand that you've created all the big deals that keep you in a separated state. Here are just a few of the typical, familiar big deals:

- "I can't afford my taxes."
- "Modern politics are ruining the country."
- "The system is rigged against me."
- "I have to go to court."
- "He didn't text me!"
- "I didn't get the job."
- "I lost my driver's license."

You believe such problems are real, buying into them and giving away your power. It appears that something is happening outside yourself, and you worry about it day in and day out, even lose sleep over it.

You may be thinking: *But my problems are really happening! I have to deal with them. They exist!* I used to feel that way, too, until I began to look past the *form* of things and see the bigger picture. Gradually, I became aware that if I kept believing in the form of all my problems, I was going to keep losing my peace and never get it back.

The good news is that even though it seems that we have separated from God, we are still *with* God and *in* God. Our Father holds us in such high regard that he would never ever make this sick, sad, depressing world real for us. You might consider it God's will that we must suffer in order to learn and grow, but is this what a truly loving parent would do?

According to the Course, God is not some faraway divine person who sits in judgment of us and doles out punishments or rewards. God is simply the capacity for perfect love that is always within each of us. Forgetting God means forgetting who we really are. Forgetting ourselves means looking at the world through the eyes of fear, when we have the choice of looking through the eyes of love. Looking out with fear is very common, but it's not compulsory!

The Solution to Our Problems

The way to solve problems begins with understanding where they are *not*. Our problems are not "out there" in the world; they are in our mind. When we believe our problems are out there, they will rapidly grow in number and intensity until it feels like we are living in hell. Hell is not some awful place where God sends people for being bad; hell is unhappiness, right where we are right now. To *live our happy*, we have to face all our big deals and forgive them. In other words, we let go of all the crap we keep telling ourselves. The simple fact is that we create all of our own experiences, and we can start creating better ones right now.

For instance, in 2009, four years after I got married, I became a divorce statistic. At the beginning, I felt a lot of loss and sadness, and I did not deny those feelings. I let myself cry, vent, and even scream! The same year, I began my studies at Pathways of Light, where I went to heal my pain about my lost marriage. The Pathways material helped me deal more effectively with my feelings by teaching me to give them over to my *inner guidance*, which we'll look at more closely in the next chapter.

Pathways and the Course eventually got me unhooked from thinking, *Oh, this is such a big deal — I am getting a divorce, and my life is over!* I began to release the big deal through accepting what I felt, and then giving all of it over to something bigger: God. I couldn't heal all by myself; I needed inside help. That help enabled me to avoid self-destructive thinking, such as: *Something is wrong with me because I am about to get divorced.*

Shift in Perception

The Course defines a *miracle* as a "shift in perception," meaning that we choose to see things in a different way. Once I had allowed myself to feel the initial pain of my divorce, I was able to make some choices about how to see it. These "shifts in perception" included the following:

- I chose to see how much I grew in the relation-ship, how it made me both more humble and more confident.
- I chose to see how it taught me what true team-work is.
- I chose to see that loving my husband meant being willing to let him go to find his happiness (and then I could, too).
- I chose to see that we both became better people because of our marriage.
- I chose to appreciate that now we have the ability to extend more love to the world because of our growth together.

Finally, the most beautiful gift of my "big deal" divorce was that it brought me to find my purpose. Seeking healing after my divorce led me to Pathways, where I began studying to become a minister — which was definitely not in my life plan before I married!

This is how I learned one of the great lessons of my spiritual life: Extraordinary gifts can be hidden in events that appear to be hard or ugly. To look for a miracle means facing those dark places in yourself where you still need to heal. Then you can learn to let go of the barriers that keep you from recognizing *the love that you are* — that is, God within. This means recognizing the "divine order" in even the most difficult challenges of your life. You have to allow for a miraculous shift in perception to see that order, so you can *live your happy*!

Here's a lesser "big deal" that still taught me something valuable. I once received a letter from the Internal Revenue Service informing me that my corporate taxes were late and that a penalty would be assessed. If I refused or didn't meet the deadline, I was threatened with fines, garnishing of my bank account, even jail. Yikes! I was ready to freak out, but by this time I had some practice in not allowing big deals to upset me.

Instead of buying into all the threats and reacting with fear, I simply sat down and wrote a calm, factual letter to the IRS explaining that I was not aware of the filing deadline, as my accountant had not alerted me that it was earlier than my personal filing. Then I dropped worrying about it. Within a couple of months I received a letter notifying me that the penalty would not be assessed on a first-time offense. Because I didn't fall for my own fears, the IRS suddenly turned nice!

Please note: The key is to *be happy* no matter the outcome. If I had received opposite news from the IRS, I would have reminded myself that the real problem was within, and then let go of thinking it was such a big deal. Then I could have dealt with whatever I needed to do in joy.

In short, there is a way to keep doing the happy dance no matter what happens.... *Rumbaaa lalala rumbaaa!*

Practice: Facing Your "Big Deals"

Now I would like you to write a list of all the nasty feelings of fear, lack, guilt, and insecurity that you may suffer from. To get started, ask yourself these three questions:

1. What major problems are you experiencing right now?
2. What outcomes do you fear?
3. What thoughts make you sad?

As you describe these troubles and challenges, follow these four rules:

1. Be as raw and honest as you can be.
2. Don't try to be too "spiritual" about what you really feel and think.
3. Be gentle with yourself.
4. Trust the process.

Many of my clients have some difficulty with these rules, especially number 2 if they are devoted to being religious or spiritual. People resist looking at difficult feelings by saying:

- "I don't want to feel those feelings because they are in the past, and I have been praying and meditating."
- "What's the point of feeling those feelings? I don't like them."

- "I don't want to look at any ugly thoughts because it is not who I am now."

However, there is nothing spiritual about withholding feelings and brushing things under the rug. Pretending that we're happy is not the same as being happy!

Make your list of "big deals," and don't hold back. We will work with this list in the next chapter!

SUMMARY OF KEY POINTS

- We typically suffer from a combination of societal expectations and personal guilt.
- The pressures and guilt we feel can make it seem as if we have an overload of problems.
- There is really only one problem: the idea that we separated from God, or the Love within that is our true nature.
- We stay separated and unhappy by making some of our problems into "big deals" that seem impossible to overcome.
- The key to solving all our problems is recognizing that they are not "out there," but within our own mind.
- We can choose to see our "big deals" differently; deciding to shift our perception is what *A Course in Miracles* calls a "miracle."
- To start seeing your problems differently, you have to be honest about them, while also being gentle with yourself — and not too "spiritual"!

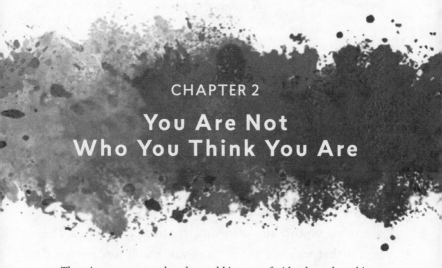

CHAPTER 2

You Are Not Who You Think You Are

There is no statement that the world is more afraid to hear than this:
I do not know the thing I am, and therefore do not know what I am doing,
where I am, or how to look upon the world or on myself.

— *ACIM*, chapter 31, section V

We can choose to see the world through the eyes of love or through the eyes of fear. This is the fundamental choice of our everyday life. In the terms of *A Course in Miracles*, this means deciding between the thought systems of the *Holy Spirit* or the *ego*. The whole world as we experience it exists because most people choose ego — the way of fear — most of the time. That is, we tend to think that we are separate, alone, unworthy, and guilty. Please excuse my Spanish if I suggest that this is all a bunch of *caca*!

In fact, I call the ego our "cuckoo" voice: It's the part of the mind that worries, judges, fears, and holds grudges. In short, the ego is out to kill our happy. The good news is that another completely different way of thinking is available to us. The Holy Spirit is right there inside our minds, waiting for the chance to remind us that happiness is our divine right! We have the power to choose freedom, and even though we may forget we have that choice, we always have more opportunities to choose love. The patience and kindness of the Holy Spirit never go away. Whenever we drift away, the Holy Spirit just waits for our return.

We drift because the ego can be very powerful. It convinces us of two simultaneous, contradictory ideas: The first is that we're unworthy, unlovable, and just not good enough; and the second is that we'll somehow find happiness out in the world, even though we don't really deserve it. Thus, our ego convinces us that if we somehow find the perfect job or relationship, we'll be happy. If we put tons of cash in the bank, we'll be happy. If we graduate from college, get a promotion, and so on, we'll be happy. But as the Course puts it so bluntly: "The ego's rule is, 'Seek but do not find' [and] 'Try to learn but do not succeed'" (*ACIM*, ch. 12, section V). Obviously, there's just no way to win with this thought system.

Your Happy Comes from Within

We have two teachers we can choose from. Depending on which thought system we choose, we are literally deciding whether to live in hell (where ego takes us) or heaven (the Holy Spirit's neighborhood). These are not places in the afterlife; they are the ways we experience existence right now.

We will experience our existence exactly as we choose: "Your picture of the world can only mirror what is within. The source of neither light nor darkness can be found without" (*ACIM*, workbook lesson 73).

For example, when I was going through my divorce, my ex-husband once called to express some anger that left me feeling very sad. My ego reaction came up right away: *Who does he think he is? What a jerk! Poor me! I haven't done anything wrong. He should be paying me alimony....* Blah blah blah. After a while I caught on, looked at where my thoughts were taking me, and began to pray: "Holy Spirit, I am feeling very sad. All my thoughts are hurting me now. I must have chosen wrongly, so now I choose again. Heal my mind, Holy Spirit — I want peace instead of this."

To my surprise, a stillness came over me right away. Soon I even began laughing. I realized that what I was thinking was just coming from my ego, the fear-driven part of my mind, and that I did not need to buy into it! I remembered this principle of the Course: *Whatever you accept into your mind has reality for you. It is your acceptance of it that makes it real.* The rest of my day was wonderful!

The Four Tricks of the Ego

Why do we choose the madness that is the ego? It's simple:

- We believe it's us.
- We don't know how not to.
- Our minds are undisciplined.

We forget our innate goodness, leading us to believe what the ego says. The Holy Spirit is the part of the mind that reminds us of the truth, which is that we are created by Love itself (also known as God). The Holy Spirit is our direct line to God. By forgetting that we are created from Love and thus are part of God, we fall asleep to our own reality. The Holy Spirit knows this and can help us wake up if we so choose.

The key to waking up is to understand the ego's tricks — that is, the tricks we play on ourselves. Let's look at the four major ones.

Ego Trick 1: The Shoulds

The ego has a favorite theme: *shoulda, coulda, woulda*. As in:

"I shoulda done this better."
"I coulda gotten that job."
"If I'd followed my hunch, things woulda worked
    out differently."

Not only does the ego use "should" to punish us inwardly with such judgments, it then projects them outward onto others:

"If you loved me, you would do so-and-so."
"You should have done things my way, then it all
    would have worked out."
"You could be doing more for this relationship."

Whether we're punishing ourselves or others, there's no winning the ego's game. We will only end up feeling disappointed and frustrated with ourselves and others. When you have these ego-programmed expectations, you can't be happy because you are too busy worrying about what the other person should be doing, instead of recognizing the real cause of your frustration: yourself.

Also, having expectations is not being loving; it's actually the opposite. You are not allowing others to be as they are, but instead imposing your ideas of how they should be. This is a trick of the ego that will always take you to hell. It's best to focus on healing our own mind, letting go of expectations, and *trusting* — a subject we will address at the end of this book. Trust is vital to *living your happy*.

Ego Trick 2: Obsession with the Past

The ego likes to keep us in the past, thinking about how we messed everything up and how we could've done it better! Our mistakes seem to be the source of our guilt, but in fact guilt always begins with the choice of separateness, as I explain in chapter 1. We actually feel guilty because we fear love even as we go around looking for it, and so we settle for its opposite.

For instance, after her breakup with her boyfriend, a client once told me that she wished that she had not acted as if she had cared so much while they had been together. By "caring" she meant acting jealous of the attention he had received from an ex. Had she not acted jealous in the past, she kept repeating, then they might still be together. She was stuck in the past, regretting that she had not lied about her real feelings! This is just one example of the ego's delusional thought system, convincing us that real love is impossible, so we might as well settle for some variety of guilt instead.

Whenever we focus on the past in a negative way, this is a choice we are making.

Ego Trick 3: Focus on the Body

Above all, the ego believes in separation, and the body is the ultimate proof that each of us is separate, different from everyone else, and thus special. Serving the body, taking care of the body, and finding distraction and pleasure through the body are the ego's preoccupations. In fact, we tend to believe that happiness is found through taking the best possible care of the body. Yet the body is more often our "problem center," especially if we are trying to find fulfillment, purpose, and intimacy through it.

Great sex, for instance, is not a bad thing, but just how often is it reliably great? How many times have you felt terrible after having sex with someone when you knew it was not a good idea — as in so-called makeup sex? In my marriage, physical intimacy was a major issue, so after we divorced, sex was all I wanted. My hurt ego convinced me that I would be happy again if I had enough sex, yet all the "hunt" brought me was sadness. I might feel good for a hot second, driving home from some guy's place, but soon I just felt empty.

Now my experience of the body is totally different because I use it to extend love, rather than try to find love through someone else's body. Let me repeat that: *I use my body to extend love*. I ask myself, how may I serve *with* this body? How can I serve *through* this body? Now I use this body to collaborate with other teachers, giving a talk, workshop, or sermon. My body is an instrument, which means that it's not who I am. It's there to serve me and others, not the other way around.

Ego Trick 4: Your Happiness Is "Out There"

When ego is running the show, you need to make things happen, and so you try to manipulate the world even if it kills you! The ego is always whispering in your ear (and it's pretty loud — what in showbiz we call a "stage whisper"), telling you that you will not be happy or free until you get enough money, or the right person, or the perfect job. If that were true, then we would not hear so many stories of people who "have it made" on a material level but who are also alcoholics, drug addicts, or suicidally depressed. The truth is that nothing "out there" will ever give you freedom or happiness. That's because you already have it — it's your divine right to be happy as a perfect child of God.

It's vital to understand the ego's tricks, which describe how the ego projects fear. Then we can recognize the ego whenever it becomes active in our minds. We must also build a relationship with our internal teacher, the Holy Spirit, so that we give to it all our false, negative thoughts, which are of no use. This is your job if you want to *live your happy*! Each day you have the opportunity to remember that you are *not* your ego thoughts; you *are* the decision maker who can choose a different way of thinking. As *A Course in Miracles* puts it: "Each day, each hour and minute, even each second, you are deciding between the crucifixion and the resurrection; between the ego and Holy Spirit. The ego is the choice for guilt; the Holy Spirit is the choice for guilt-lessness" (*ACIM*, ch. 14, section III).

Stop, Look, and Listen

How can you remember who you really are? First, by becoming aware of your thoughts. Know who is running the show! You can learn to recognize the cuckoo voice and all its negative chatter, but it is *muy importante* to be mindful! Here is the process I use:

1. Stop: Take a deep breath and pause to notice what you're thinking and feeling. If your mind is running loose with negative chatter, just *stop it*!

2. Look: Now, look at your thought patterns. *S-l-o-w d-o-w-n* the pace of your thoughts so that it is easier to notice when the cuckoo voice is blocking your inner wisdom.

3. Ask and listen: Ask to see difficult situations or people in another way. When your cuckoo voice has quieted, you can begin to hear the voice of the Holy Spirit telling you how to shift your perceptions. Trust that you will receive the insights that will bring you to your happy!

Okay, now get ready to do some work. True change happens when we work at it! We tend to let our minds wander too much, and learning to discipline our minds is the key to ending suffering. So think of the following practice as an aerobic exercise for your mind.

Practice: Ego Release

Return to the list you created in chapter 1 that details your negative thoughts (from the "Facing Your 'Big Deals'" practice). In this practice, you're going to surrender this list to the Holy Spirit and ask to receive guidance. Remember, this is not about being "spiritual" but being honest and vulnerable. It might hurt to review your negative thinking; you might sweat and even cry! But keep at it, feel your feelings, and vent whatever you need to. Remember, you are asking for help. This is where you begin to build the Holy Spirit muscle in your mind.

First, review your list of cuckoo thoughts from the previous exercise, and then write the following in your journal: "Holy Spirit, I don't know what any of this means. I want to see this differently because I want to be happy. I surrender all these fears to you — show me the way!"

Then, start freewriting, trusting that the Holy Spirit has heard you and will show the way. Even if it does not make sense, just write and keep writing! Take as much time as you need. You may be surprised at the new and healing thoughts that come to you. The Holy Spirit is good and powerful and won't let you down.

To show you how this works, here is an example of how I did this exercise myself in my journal. First, I've reproduced my "ego rant" — the list of all the cuckoo thoughts (from the chapter 1 practice) that I knew were blocking my happy:

- I have had four auditions, and I have not even booked one!
- I did not say the monologue the way I wanted to.
- I have a theatrical agent, and I don't get any theatrical auditions. I have a hosting agent, and I don't get any hosting auditions.
- I have not met anyone I like.
- If I like Chris, he has to make money so he can provide for me.
- Why can't I live in a better neighborhood?!!!
- I am sad, I feel lonely. Why can't I find someone I like?!!!
- I am worried I will never get married again and not get to experience being a mother, that breaks my heart. I thought I would get to be a mother. Why do other people get to have children? And I can't even have the opportunity to? This makes me so sad!
- I do not feel worthy.
- I am not lovable.

After writing out this rant, I surrendered it to the Holy Spirit, and this is the message I received, which I also wrote in my journal:

- Wanting things to be different is what makes you sad. Accept and know that things are exactly perfect and that you are always only a thought away from feeling good!

- Not being in a relationship is actually saving you from much suffering. The only way you can experience the love of God is by appearing to be single at the moment. This is the best way for your learning now. You are healing, and I am here with you.
- You have Sophie and Sasha right here in your living room. For now, you are a mother to two furry girls.
- Be patient and loving with yourself. All is being taken care of. Trust.
- You can feel happy if you truly want to. It's up to you.
- I am grateful for your courage to heal your mind and for being willing to come back to me.

When I do exercises such as this, something becomes very clear for me that may become clear for you: *You are not an ego, and you are not a body.* You are a perfect spirit who has the capacity to choose your happy! You might find it difficult to let go of your ego rants at first, or it may seem that the Holy Spirit is not answering you. If so, it's important to remember that unhappiness is a habit that can become very familiar — and that familiarity can make unhappiness seem inevitable. It takes work to undo any kind of bad habit, especially habits of mind. Even if the Holy Spirit's responses are not clear at first, keep at it (and see the next chapter for more inspiration). As time goes by, you will find another way of thinking, relating, and being.

SUMMARY OF KEY POINTS

- We can choose to hear the voice of fear or the voice of love. The ego is the voice of fear; the Holy Spirit is the voice of love.
- Your happy comes from within, not "out there."
- The ego uses some powerful tricks to keep us looking "out there."
- You can *stop, look, ask, and listen* to undo the ego's tricks.
- You can ask the Holy Spirit to help you see your problems differently.
- You are not an ego, and you are not a body.

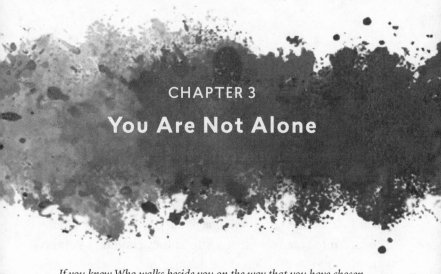

CHAPTER 3

You Are Not Alone

*If you knew Who walks beside you on the way that you have chosen,
fear would be impossible.*

— *ACIM*, chapter 18, section III

I am sure that at some point in your life, you have felt sad and alone, as if it were just you against the world. Perhaps you've had thoughts like these:

"It's so hard getting through the day sometimes, feeling like I have no help."

"I'm too scared to be on my own."

"I just can't do this alone."

Well, if you are counting on your "own" strength — that is, your ego strength — you have every right to feel scared and alone. As I've said, the ego is no *bueno* and unreliable. When you identify with your ego, you will always end up feeling helpless and alone. As *A Course in Miracles* puts it:

"The presence of fear is a sure sign that you are trusting in your own strength" (*ACIM*, workbook lesson 48).

In my early twenties, right before I booked my gig with the World Wrestling Federation, I experienced some major fear. Even though I had already been working as an actress and TV host, I suffered from major insecurity issues and was constantly worried about the future. I was always asking myself: *Will I make it as an actress? Will I be successful? What will I do for the rest of my life? What's my purpose?* Doubt turned into fear, fear turned into sadness, and that sadness turned into depression. I remember how shocked I was when my parents told me I was depressed. I didn't think depression could happen to just anyone, and especially not to me! I was stunned and very angry. Why the hell didn't they teach me about this in school?!

Since then, I've come to understand what that depression was really about: *I felt alone.* Not that I was by myself. I had plenty of people around me — loving parents and caring friends. The loneliness was in my mind and caused by what I call the "It's All about Me" Syndrome: *Me, me, me! I have to do this all by myself. I have to make everything happen! Everything is a big deal!* In short, my life, my problems, and my career defined me.

This way of life is no fun, and it's really exhausting. Suffering and fear can feel endless when it seems like you have to make everything happen on your own.

Why You Are Not Alone

Most of us do experience ourselves as "separate." We believe we are trapped in bodies, each of us with special interests and unique circumstances that appear to make our separation very real. This makes us feel vulnerable, sometimes to the extent of identifying ourselves as victims struggling against a world of sadness, sickness, and ultimately death. We are fascinated by the world, which so convinces us of our separateness that we forget the truth: *We are not alone.*

Everyone has the Voice of God within. This voice goes by many names: inner wisdom, inner guide, the light within, your true self, your right mind. I suggest you use whatever name feels right to you. Before I begin my "Accessing Inner Wisdom" sessions with clients, I ask them what they'd like to call their inner guide. They may say Jesus or God, or simply "the Light." There is no wrong way to identify your constant inner companion, and you may even change your name for it over time. Regardless, this inner companion or voice is always loving, gentle, and certain, and it can lead you back to your happy place!

It's that part of our mind that knows we all are one. It does not judge, but loves unconditionally. It's not concerned with "getting" because it knows we have everything within. When you are aware of your inner companion, you will experience a flowing ease and grace. The resolution of all your problems comes from experiencing this grace, since when you do, you solve the only real problem you have: the idea that somehow, once upon a time, you separated from God. The Holy Spirit — *ACIM*'s name for the inner companion — helps us let go of our attachment to the world of form. The more we can do that, the more we experience our oneness with God. When you allow this to happen, your whole life will change. You will experience much gratitude and joy!

As the Course says, "God is your safety in every circumstance. His voice speaks for him at all situations and in every aspect of all situations, telling you exactly what to do to call upon his strength and his protection. There are no exceptions because God has no exceptions. And the voice which speaks for him thinks as he does" (*ACIM*, workbook lesson 47).

Experiencing Aloneness and Its Opposite

I became a host for the World Wrestling Federation after winning an audition over five hundred other young women. You would think I would feel so happy: *¡Gracias Dios mío! This is the gig of a lifetime, national TV and such a prestigious company.…* But I was in the middle of the depression I described above; I was a hot mess, and I still got the job! Sometimes we create experiences to feed our growth, and we don't necessarily have to be in a happy place to manifest them. There was a reason for this job, and I was going to have to live it and learn from it.

I did learn — by suffering a lot. Because I had no sense of an inner companion to bear me through difficulties, I felt as if I was not worthy of the job, even though I won a tough audition. I was insecure about my Spanish because my accent is Cuban, and Mexican is preferred on Spanish TV. On top of that, WWF shows were filmed live, meaning that any mistake I made would be seen live by thousands. On my very first show, I remember going down the ramp in front of twenty thousand people while I listened to an earphone as the director told me, "Maria, get out there and interview the wrestlers next to the ring, then come back up the ramp with them." It felt like *mi corazón* was coming out of my chest!

This was such a challenge, not because of the job itself, but because I thought I had to succeed all on my own. I went on to do fifty episodes and worked with such amazing talents as El Hijo del Santo, Negro Casas, Papi Chulo, The Rock, Stone Cold Steve Austin — and, let's not forget, a midget wrestler named Mini Max, who was my scripted love crush on the show. Despite all the attention and seeming success, my almost paralyzing insecurities continued throughout this amazing gig. I spent a lot of time on tour in my hotel rooms getting on my knees, praying to God, and reading the Bible.

Looking back on all that, I recognize that sometimes our deepest pains bring us closer to God so that we can learn and grow. With spiritual maturity, I have discovered that I can learn through joy, without the need for so much pain.

In early 2012 I was asked to start the Spanish ministry at Unity Burbank Center for Spiritual Awareness in California. At first I was a bit scared, thinking: *I don't know how to run a ministry, and I am not even a minister yet.* I wasn't set to be ordained until November. Even though I was anxious, I was open and willing to hear that still small voice within me that said *yes*! So I stepped into the position and began to create a program and find musicians. I would constantly ask the Holy Spirit for help, and my goal was always to feel joy through the process. I am not going to say I did not feel nervous when I gave my first talk — although it quickly went away when I remembered: *This is not about "me," Maria the separated self who must be perfect.* No, this time the opportunity was *all about us* — that is, an opportunity to extend love and remember that I am not alone.

Our suffering increases whenever our mind-set is self-centered, focusing on thoughts like *what can I get, how can I get them to like me, how can I keep this job*, and so on. In our struggle to "make a name" for ourselves, stake our claim, and prove our individual worth, we make the separation real and condemn ourselves to loneliness and misery. By contrast, when we regard whatever we're doing as a kind of ministry — focusing on thoughts like *what can I give, how can I be of service, how will my actions benefit everyone* — then we will inevitably experience joy and happiness. Another way of expressing this truth is that *all that is real is love.*

How to Listen to the Holy Spirit

First, the Holy Spirit will always meet you where you are. That's because it's always with you in the first place. Our inner wisdom never really leaves us, but we still find ways to forget this!

Here are four effective ways you can snap back to the truth, back into the arms of your true guide:

1. Try BIG willingness. The Course advises that we need only "a little willingness" to forgive and open our minds, and the rest of the process takes care of itself. Willingness simply means being open to the possibility of change. In my experience, one benefits

the most from BIG willingness. We tend to be entranced by our grievances, which I discuss next. So it can take some real effort to change your mind.

2. Choose peace. When you are in a state of peace, you give the Holy Spirit permission to shine its light in your mind. This is why it's important to choose peace in every circumstance. For instance, when you have a job interview, you can go into it thinking, *I want peace*, instead of *I've got to have this job.* Or instead of thinking, *I've got to make more money*, remember *I want peace.* This reorientation of your thinking takes your attention from the world "out there" and brings you within, where your true power resides.

3. Stay attuned to signs and symbols. The Holy Spirit sometimes works in mysterious ways. It may not send you big "answers" so much as helpful coincidences, unexpected meetings, or not-so-subtle messages in songs, movies, or books that cross your path at exactly the right time. So pay attention, and be vigilant for signs of hope and change. Your true Self is always ready to be found, and the Holy Spirit will send you some pretty interesting pointers on your search.

4. Practice, practice, practice. As you consistently ask your inner guide for help, the connection to spirit will get stronger and stronger. Your trust will build. If you practice getting out of your own way by forgiving and letting go, it will become easier for the Holy Spirit to guide you all the time.

Letting Go of What You're Not

Another cause of feeling alone and helpless is the common attachment to *grievances*. Anytime you are unhappy, you can be sure you're holding on to some kind of grievance or resentment. Whenever you are judging anyone or anything, you're holding a grievance. This negative holding enhances an unconscious condition of separation, making you feel more alone. This can lead to a life of chronic unhappiness and sorrow; it's really like a slow death.

Workbook lesson 168 from the Course, "Love holds no grievances," offers this explanation: "You who were created by love like itself can hold no grievances and know your self." That means that keeping a grievance is holding on to something that's *not you*.

Here's a basic process for letting go of what you're not, so you can discover the happiness and power within that's your birthright.

Practice: Releasing Grievances

Close your eyes and bring to mind, one by one, everyone you hold a grievance against, whether the grievance is big or small. Every grievance disturbs your peace of mind equally. Try to see each person as your best friend, using thoughts like these: *I see you as a dear friend, I see you as light, and I see you as part of me. As I see your truth, I awaken to mine.*

Then, in your mind, step back and imagine a circle of everyone you have brought to mind, with everyone holding hands. Feel the sense of peace that has been created. Feel the safety of the love that's holding you up. Just let yourself be in this new, accepting space within your mind for a little while. Afterward, you will notice that you feel lighter, more peaceful.

Do this exercise often to help heal your grievances. You gotta work it, since we all get used to bad habits of holding onto grievances and resentments.

Remembering the Truth

I also find it helpful when I remember *who I am in truth* beneath all the daily concerns and anxieties that can crop up. One way to experience your inner truth is to write a letter from the point of view of your best and deepest self. Writing this letter is best done while sitting in a quiet place where you can feel unhurried. Here is a letter I wrote when I was doing my ministerial studies at Pathways of Light:

Dear Maria,

You are a loving perfect child of God. Your soul dwells in truth. You can remember, dear child, that you are not your limiting beliefs or past bonds. I am here to remind you that you are free from any bonds: your soul is lovable, joyful, and peaceful. Your unconditional love reaches others like you can't even imagine. You see people as God sees them; that is your gift! As you see the truth in others, you recognize it in yourself. I'm so proud of you. You've come a long way. I am proud of your commitment. I love you! Continue to spread your joy and your gift of speaking, of making a difference. Your charisma and beauty are extraordinary; use them as a tool to extend love and truth. Your stand in the truth is immeasurable. Don't underestimate yourself; you are ahead many hours and days. You have saved yourself much time of suffering, and I say this to you on firm ground. Continue the process; it's working, dear child. Awakening is taking place, and I'm so proud of you! You will start to see yourself as I see you: confident, loving, kind, and humble, making a difference! Maria, you are free from your past, you are free from this point forward. You have become a master, an angel from the sky who knows she has never separated from her father. Dear child, I am so proud of you. Remember, you're never alone. I am always with you.

Practice: Staying Present

We may think we feel alone because we don't have a partner, spouse, or family. Or perhaps we feel the world hasn't treated us right or our lives just feel out of control. As this chapter has explained, we feel alone when we depend only on our own strength, when we hold on to grievances, and when we don't listen for inner guidance. To overcome these popular habits of mind, we have to work at it. Here are useful exercises to practice daily, some for morning and some for night:

Each morning:

- Pray for guidance. Ask the Holy Spirit: "What would You have me do? Where would You have me go? What would You have me say, and to whom?"

- Write out your intentions, such as: "My intention today is to be present," or "My intention today is to remember I can choose happiness."

- Ask yourself: "What do I want? What would I like to feel? What would I like to experience today?"

- Give over your day to the Holy Spirit. Say to yourself: "Holy Spirit, I give you this day. I put it in your hands, knowing I am safe and always cared for."

Every night:

- Pray for peace: "I ask for peace of mind, knowing it's my divine right as a child of God."

- Write about what you are grateful for. Start a gratitude journal, noting not only the good circumstances of your life but also your inner gifts: "I am grateful that I can choose peace of mind. I am grateful to know God loves me."

- Release the day: "I let go of this day. It's been exactly perfect."

- Give your sleep over to the Holy Spirit: "Whatever needs to be healed, may it be healed as I sleep. I give over my sleep to You, so that I sleep with the angels."

SUMMARY OF KEY POINTS

- Everyone has the Voice of God within. It goes by many names: inner wisdom, inner guide, the light within, your true self, your right mind.
- It may require BIG willingness to change your mind.
- Always choose peace first.
- The Holy Spirit will meet you where you are at.
- Anytime you are unhappy, you can be sure you're holding on to some kind of grievance; whenever you are judging anyone or anything in your mind, you're holding a grievance.
- A daily practice can help you stay present.

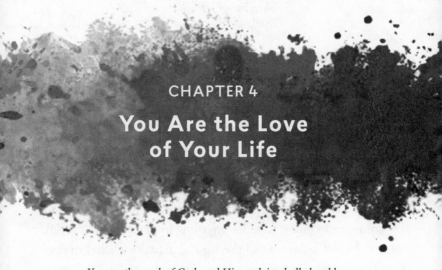

CHAPTER 4

You Are the Love of Your Life

You are the work of God, and His work is wholly lovable and wholly loving. This is how a man must think of himself in his heart, because that is what he is.

— *ACIM*, chapter 1, section III

When we are always looking for something or someone to complete us, we soon feel as if we're living in hell. Happiness and love go hand in hand, and we are taught that not only our happiness but also our love are somewhere "out there." Some of these thoughts and attitudes may sound familiar:

> "I must get all I can from the outside world because I feel empty inside."
>
> "When I have enough stuff, I'll be happy."
>
> "I eat too much because it distracts me from feeling unloved."
>
> "I must do well at school or work so I'm praised enough to feel good."

"I must find a lover or mate who makes me feel worthwhile."

That last one was me! I was looking for love in all the wrong places, especially in the wrong men. I made men my God, and I suffered a lot in the process. Because we choose to be separate from the God within, we all suffer from the syndrome of unworthiness in one way or another. When we don't feel worthy of even existing, we look for something or someone to give it to us — anything to make us feel special.

In fact, what we call the "ego" is actually a belief in specialness. When we forget that we are one with God — which means a state of inner security, stability, and happiness that far surpasses feeling special — then we won't be able to feel love within, and we'll settle for the ego's substitutes instead. That's when we need something or someone to make us feel special.

This is summed up well in one of the Pathways of Light courses called "Special Relationship vs. Holy Relationship" (practitioner course 905):

> In truth, love in this world of bodies really means, "I want to be special, but I also feel alone, lacking and unworthy, which I can't stand. Will you be my special partner and promise to keep your body around and help me feel special? This will help submerge my pangs of loneliness, lack, and unworthiness. I will get the specialness, acknowledgment, and attention I want so desperately. In return I will shower you with specialness. I will agree to give you special attention and shower you with my exclusive

'love.' Then through our allegiance in being special partners, we will avoid the side-effects of loneliness and guilt that our desire for specialness brings. We will be happy our own way, in our little world of specialness. We will be each other's idols and re-place the Love of God."

When I read this I thought, "*Dios mío,* this is what I have been doing all my life!"

I will share a personal story about this below, but first let's discuss the first step of self-love: accepting everything you feel.

Feeling Your Feelings

Feeling your fear, worry, sadness, and other negative feelings with the same openness that you feel confidence or a good mood is the beginning of accepting all of yourself, and is a beautiful act of self-love. Facing hard feelings can be uncomfortable, but instead of rejecting or running away from them, you can transform them by letting them be just as they are.

For example, I've been working with a student named Carly for several years, and she once sent me this text:

Hey, Maria. I just wanted to reach out — answer this when/if you have time. I just got a new job yesterday, and put in my two weeks' notice at my current job. I am feeling so sad and down, even though I know this is a good thing, and I am going to a place that's closer to my house and pays a higher salary. I am making this so real and feel so sad. I am not sure what to do!

Here was my response:

Hi — Congratulations! What a joy! New beginnings!!! It feels to me like you're resisting being sad, as if something is wrong with that. It's a natural thing that happens. Since we are in the body, we get sad, upset about worldly stuff. Our job is always to be aware that we are choosing to be sad and give it over to the Holy Spirit. Remember, you don't have to do anything with your behavior; the change that counts is always in your mind.

I was sad and scared when I moved to where I am now, my new place. It was more expensive than my old place, where I was in my comfort zone and had memories with my ex-husband. But I let myself go through those feelings and did my spiritual practice.

This is a beautiful transition for you, enjoy it! Even if you're sad. Be with the sadness, and I know since you live a life of trust it shall pass, as you choose to do so.

I hope this helped!

Here was how Carly replied:

Wow, Maria, thank you. You are right! I can allow myself to be sad and feel my feelings through this job transition. Just knowing this actually made me feel much better. I was definitely making myself wrong and bad for feeling sad, and I wanted to change how I felt. It's so helpful to remember that my feelings aren't bad, and that even though I'm doing a spiritual practice, that doesn't mean that my feelings go away. They are still there, but now I can take what I'm feeling to the Holy Spirit. It's crazy to think that I can trust and enjoy this even though I feel sad! But that's not actually crazy, that's really sanity, right? That's what living *A Course in Miracles* means. I'm going to let myself feel this and bring it to the Holy Spirit. Thank you for seeing me in high regard and for your love and support!

You can use *all* your feelings as a tool to awaken. Whatever life brings you is just enough to bring you home to yourself.

Awaking from My Slow Death

I have experienced this dynamic personally. For a long time in my life, if I did not have a boyfriend, I was not happy. I needed to be with another body, and I needed constant comforting and recognition, which I called "love." If I did not have this, I was a hot mess. A man was more important than my job and even my family. I was constantly searching for the perfect man to marry and have children with, and I hardly noticed that this search made me miserable.

Looking back, I can see that I was attacking my true

self: the love of God within me. That love is eternal and can never die, but if you're always turning away from it, you feel as if you're dying inside.

This predicament finally began to change in 2014, when I met "the Buddha guy." He was so handsome: tall, dark hair, beautiful tanned skin, great body. Not only was he eye candy, he was *spiritual* — a practicing Buddhist who chanted every day! Oh, and he had his own thriving business. We had a couple of dates that went well, and I was beginning to really like him. Then he brought up a slight issue: There were some other young women "taking up real estate" in his mind, as he put it. My immediate reaction was: So why was he dating me?! I wanted to choke him, but I didn't, though I did slam a few kitchen cabinets while we discussed this issue. Finally, I did something new for me. I said, "I am done, get out."

Shocked, he replied, "You want me to leave?" I repeated that yes, I did. This stance was *muy importante* because, in the past, I would have tried to fix things no matter what, even if it meant settling for a situation that was unhealthy. After ending our relationship, I felt sad for the next few days, and I yearned to text or call, thinking it would calm my pain, but I resisted the urge. This taught me that I am not just my feelings, and I don't have to be controlled by them. I have the choice to "rest in God" instead, an internal state that guarantees happiness.

This state is what I call a true love affair with everyone and everything. In this condition, you recognize that giving and receiving are one. You extend love rather than trying to get it. That means that, when you are close to someone, you can be raw, authentic, and honest. You reveal your "baggage" instead of hiding it, as the ego wants to do. You are willing to heal with another, instead of using hurt feelings to enforce separation. Most important, you realize that every relationship has only one true purpose: to awaken to God. Together, you both ask, "How may this relationship serve? What is it for?"

Becoming Ready to Be Happy

You might be wondering what happened. What changed that allowed me to recognize I was the love of my life? The truth is, before this happened, I really did not have any idea how my mind worked. I was studying the Course and other perspectives, but I was not *experiencing* what I was reading because my unconscious belief in separation prevented me from adopting a new outlook. What made the difference is that *I finally became ready to be happy*. I had to decide to choose happiness, and only I could do so; books and courses could not decide for me. We are each the decision maker in our own lives, and when we tap into that power, we are ready to rumble in miracles!

I became ready by learning to recognize when I was holding on to a grievance or looking for happiness "out there." These are both ways of telling ourselves that the God within ourselves is not real, and so we seek to be "saved" by finding some kind of solution elsewhere. With practice, I began to notice these thoughts and feelings and give them over to the Holy Spirit. I constantly practiced giving things over, even if I felt this process was not working. I would "choose again" — and again. The more I did, the more I could see a whole world inside me, so incredibly lovely and not dependent on external things. I got unhooked from the world outside, which mattered less and less.

I used this mantra: *I am the love of my life because I am God's.* Using this practice, I slowly cultivated genuine self-love, which means experiencing my true self within God. Once I felt this, having a boyfriend wasn't as important.

You can choose as well. You choose to be the love of your life when you are ready to be. That choice can take place right now. All you need to declare is "I am willing!" You make the choice for truth, the right mind, holy love, or God — whatever you want to call it. Then you start to live that choice.

Practice: Seeing Relationships Differently

Think of the relationships in your life that feel strained — where there is lots of ego and not much honesty. Write down the names of the people in these relationships. Then, take a few deep breaths and bring yourself to complete stillness. Think of each person, and as he or she passes through your mind, ask the Holy Spirit within: *What is this relationship for? How can I see it another way? How can this relationship serve love?*

Next, write down what you receive from the Holy Spirit. Don't be confused if what you're writing doesn't make sense at first. Trust the process even if it seems that you're not getting insights.

You can even write, "I am not getting insights," until you begin to feel or sense something new. This will help you get in touch with your inner wisdom. With practice and repetition, you will begin to have new insights about your most important and challenged relationships.

Love Is One

You may think there are different types of love. A love for this and a love for that; a way of loving one person and a different way of loving another. You may think that you love your child more than your best friend, or your husband more than the store clerk. But Love is one. It has no degrees and can't really be separated into different forms.

A very helpful approach is to consider that you can love *everyone*. That doesn't mean being everyone's friend, hanging out with someone you dislike, or allowing anyone to treat you badly. It means letting go of the judgments that define other people and keep you feeling separate from them. When you do that, you develop a different outlook on the world and yourself. This will increasingly deliver you into a state of grace and automatically create the experience of self-love, which is also the love of God. There is no difference in what you truly are and what the love of God is. The same love that is in God is in you and in everyone. And *that* love is the real deal!

Similar to the way you can't love someone else if you are being critical of them, you can't experience self-love if you are busy crucifying yourself. I see this problem all the time, with friends, students, and even myself. People can become very negative toward themselves if things don't work out the way they want, and they blame themselves for whatever they think they did wrong. The truth is, you can't really mess up because ultimately everything works together for the higher good.

Whenever you find yourself disappointed or unsure what to do in any relationship or situation, it is helpful to ask these questions:

Is this thought based on valuing myself?
Is this action based on valuing myself?
Is this pattern of behavior based on valuing myself?

You can also ask: If I believe that I am worthy of love, that I am complete and whole with nothing lacking, how does that mean I should think and act?

Practice: Recognizing Love

As you go about your day, anytime you meet or notice anyone, think: *We share the same love.* Then, when you see the next person, repeat in your thoughts: *We share the same love.* Whenever any person comes to mind, repeat this mantra. This new habit will help you let go of the old thinking that distinguishes types of love.

Love flows within you eternally. It's gentle and trusting; in love you do not feel lesser or better than anyone. Love sees the truth of connection beyond the everyday illusions of our seemingly separated condition. When you are filled with love, you will attract loving people, loving circumstances, and loving symbols. When you see the world from the perspective of the love within, you will experience being the love of your life because you won't see love as outside yourself. Be willing to see love in the mirror, no matter what. Then you will find that other people naturally bring out the Holy Spirit within you, instead of ego.

The following passage from *A Course in Miracles* (workbook lesson 264) offers a poetic summary of this state of being:

> Father, you stand before me and behind, beside me, in the place I see myself, and everywhere I go. You are in all the things I look upon, the sounds I hear, and every hand that reaches for my own. In You time disappears, and place becomes a meaningless belief. For what surrounds Your son and keeps him safe is love itself. There is no source but this, and nothing that does not share its holiness; that stands beyond Your one creation, or without the love which holds all things within itself. Father, Your son is like yourself. We come to You in Your own name today, to be at peace with You in your everlasting love.

To recognize that all the love you could ever want is already in you, and has never left you, means undoing the belief in separation. As the decision maker in charge of your life, you can learn to *choose love* over separation, and that unhooks you from the dream that most people are lost in. You can shine the light of love within to all your brothers and sisters by declaring: *I wish you peace, I wish you gentleness, I wish you clarity, I wish you happiness, I wish you love.* As you do, you'll find that you're also giving these blessings to yourself.

SUMMARY OF KEY POINTS

- When you are always looking for something or someone to complete you, you will soon feel as if you're living in hell.
- Ego is a belief in specialness.
- It's okay to feel all your feelings. Use them as a tool to awaken.
- You choose to be the love of your life when you are ready to be.
- Love flows within you eternally. It's gentle and trusting, and in love you do not feel lesser or better than anyone.
- You can't mess it up!

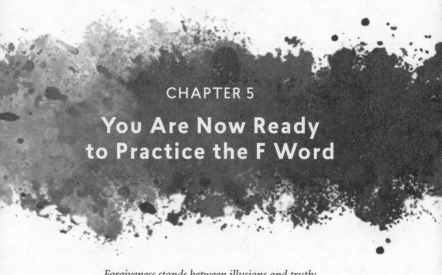

CHAPTER 5

You Are Now Ready to Practice the F Word

Forgiveness stands between illusions and truth;
between the world you see and that which lies beyond;
between the hell of guilt and Heaven's gate.

— *ACIM*, workbook lesson 134

You are now ready to practice the F word! And no, it's not what you think. What I mean is forgiveness, true forgiveness. This is not the same as worldly forgiveness, which still contains some type of judgment. We practice worldly forgiveness when we say things like: "I forgive you even though you did something wrong," or "I forgive you because I have Jesus and you don't."

No, I'm talking about the radical form of forgiveness as taught by *A Course in Miracles*. Radical forgiveness is based on this powerful idea: All that should be remembered from the past is the love we have given and received.

Before we go there, let's start with why it's *muy importante* to practice real forgiveness: It's the primary tool for getting back to *living your happy*. You forgive because you want peace, you forgive because you want joy, you forgive because you want to stop suffering. How will forgiveness do all this for you?

When we choose to believe we are separate from the Holy Spirit, and thus when we believe we are a body isolated from other bodies, guilt comes along with that choice. We don't remember making this choice, and that's why we don't understand all the guilt we feel. This is why the Course says that *we are never upset for the reasons we think*. Other people may seem to cause our problems; unfortunate life events may seem to make us unhappy; all the seemingly inevitable difficulties of life may make us feel that we've been treated unfairly. All that comes from our choice to feel separate, alone, and guilty.

We don't make that choice just once, however; we keep making it all the time without realizing what we're doing. Nor will our "normal" ego point of view ever let us in on this secret: What we give, we will ultimately receive. If we give the world our guilt, we will get back guilt. On the other hand, if we give love, we will experience love. This is why we are guided to forgive: It is our recognition that we are responsible for the way we experience other people, the world, and our life.

Judgments Kill

Here is another great reason to forgive: *Judgments kill your happy*. While judgments may make us feel temporarily more sure of ourselves, ultimately they keep us in fear, bound by the illusion of separateness. When we make *anything* out-side ourselves real, we are holding a judgment. Judgment means we have forgotten we are in the mind of God, and that will inevitably make us feel miserable. As the Course puts it, "Anger must come from judgment. Judgment is the weapon I would use against myself, to keep the miracle away from me" (*ACIM*, workbook lesson 347).

Here are some judgments I have heard from my students:

> "What kind of guy would say that he likes me and then tell me he wants to be with someone else? What a jerk!"
>
> "How can that crazy person be running for presi-dent?"
>
> "That killer/child abuser/terrorist is a bad person!"

However justified such thoughts may seem, they add to our fear and make the separation real. They mean we are buying into the ego's thought system and getting lost in illusions. Of course, it's hard not to buy into the drama, the madness, and the general BS of the ego. Our judgments *seem* to help us make sense of a crazy world. But it's worth thinking about whether judging is truly helpful and making a positive difference in one's life and the world. If a bad per-son dies, will that make you truly happy? When you watch the news and react with one judgment after another, do you end up jumping for joy or wanting to cut your veins? It's vital to realize what you are thinking because whatever you're thinking is what you put out into the world. And this will be exactly what you get back.

Whenever you are tempted to judge another person's

thoughts, beliefs, or behavior, you might find it helpful to ask yourself: Would I judge myself for this?

To get back to your happy, you must learn to hold all things in high regard, no matter the form. You must be willing to look at the battleground of the world and realize it cannot be real if only love is real. Forgiveness removes the barriers to love, so that you can begin to see the world differently. You cannot believe in love and fear at the same time.

What Is True Forgiveness?

True forgiveness can be defined in several ways:

- Forgiveness is a change of perception from fear to love.
- Forgiveness is being willing to see things another way.
- Forgiveness is letting go of the past.

Because the ego doesn't habitually think this way, forgiveness requires being willing to ask the Holy Spirit, our deepest inner wisdom, for help to see a situation or person differently. Forgiveness releases false perceptions and helps us recognize glitches in our thinking. It's hard to give up unhappy thoughts on our own, but developing a new habit of asking within for the help we need to forgive makes all the difference.

Another surprising element of true forgiveness is that *we learn to forgive people for what they did NOT do* — that is, we learn to let go of our *judgments* about everything that others do. This means that no matter what someone else seems to have done wrong, we are always letting go of our own illusions. Our fundamental shared reality is love, and anything less that we perceive — in others or within ourselves — is literally not real. The Course advises us to see anything that someone does as either an expression of love or a call for love, no matter what the person thinks they are doing. In either case, our only sensible response is love or forgiveness. Rather than taking someone else's act of cruelty or thoughtlessness as real and effective, we maintain the mindfulness to see that what was behind the action was *an attempt to get back to love.*

So be mindful! Don't make the madness of the ego's world real. Instead, let go of the false ideas that we are each separate, alone, and opposed to one another's interests. Thinking that way, you will experience major sadness and conflict and end up feeling as if you are a victim. The truth is that you are not a victim, and there is nothing being done to you. This is just an illusion that you can learn to see differently by asking the Holy Spirit within for help. Your own inner resource will turn things miraculously around, and you will feel much joy.

When to Forgive?

Any feelings that are less than happy are signals to practice the F word! For instance, practice forgiveness:

- when you are not at peace,
- when you catch yourself judging,
- when you are feeling like a victim, and
- when you are rehashing the past.

The biggest signal to forgive is when you are not feeling at peace, whether you're annoyed or angry, sad, or just feeling slightly "off." Practicing forgiveness does not mean you should pretend happiness or force yourself to feel better when you don't. However, when you feel overtaken by thoughts or emotions you don't want to have, the surest way to change your state of mind is always forgiveness.

Judging is a sure way to lose your peace. If you catch yourself making someone or something "out there" wrong, thinking you're in the right (or vice versa), it's time to forgive. You cannot be happy as long as you believe that anything happening to you is caused by something "out there" in the world. As the Course suggests, "You are not the victim of the world you see." Jesus uses the example of his own life to make the point: "I elected, for your sake and mine, to demonstrate that the most outrageous assault, as judged by the ego, does not matter. As the world judges these things, but not as God knows them, I was betrayed, abandoned, beaten, torn, and finally killed....You are not persecuted, nor was I. You are not asked to repeat my experiences because the Holy Spirit, Whom we share, makes this unnecessary" (*ACIM*, ch. 6, section I).

For sure, this is a different view than the one most of us were raised with. We are not punished by what happened to *anyone* in the past — including ourselves! The Holy Spirit is a real force within us, to whom we can always turn to remember forgiveness. And the time to remember forgiveness is always *now* — and over and over again, as much as it takes to *live our happy*!

Practice: The Forgiveness Process

To be honest, it took me years to understand true forgiveness. A way of thinking can exist for so long that it takes some time to undo what you have learned and reinforced, even when it doesn't work. So be open and trust that you will get it when you're ready.

The forgiveness process involves three steps: accept responsibility, remember what is real, and ask for help.

Accept responsibility: First, acknowledge that you create your perceptions and experience. No matter what you may be upset about, say: "I take responsibility for the way I am seeing this person or situation — through the eyes of fear or love."

Remember what is real: Any experience or feeling that is not coming from love is not real. Fear and separation are always illusions; in truth, they don't exist and never really happened. You forgive by letting go of what was never there in the first place. You forgive the person for what they did not do because they were not in their right mind. They forgot their source.

Ask for help: When you feel stuck, give over the situation to the Holy Spirit and ask for a miracle — that is, a shift in perception.

You begin the process of forgiveness simply by being willing to see the truth, looking past the deadly images of the so-called real world to what lies underneath. Every time you believe that a problem at work or at home is real and requires you to be anxious, guilty, or defensive, you can learn to *overlook* all those negative energies to see the potential of love that's hidden behind all the illusions. *You can even use feeling attacked as a way to remember to come home.* Enjoy the power of turning around your perceptions, and rejoice that you are finally waking up. Recognize fear for what it is, just a nightmare that you can choose to wake up from. You *can* choose again; forgive and you will experience heaven on earth.

The Abs Guy: My Big Forgiveness Challenge

We can be strongly tempted not to forgive when an issue in our lives seems very big or painful. Believe me, I know. I had a short-lived romance with this guy who had an amazing physique, with a six-pack of steel...*que rico!* I admit that's what hooked me. (See what happens when you make a body real?) One month after we had broken things off, I began to have sharp painful cramps. The pain would not go away, so I went to the doctor. I was shocked when she told me I might be pregnant.

I remembered the last night I was with the "Abs Guy." We had a big fight about not having used protection. He had wanted me to take the Plan B pill, which I did, and so I thought I couldn't get pregnant. Since then, I'd even had my period. At the doctor's office, I took a pregnancy test, and they told me to call the next day for the results. The next day, I was getting ready for an audition, but I was in so much pain I could not even apply my makeup. I felt as if I were going to faint. Thank goodness, I had a friend staying with me, and she helped me while I called the doctor.

The nurse told me that I might be having an ectopic pregnancy and that I had to go to the hospital. *Ectopic?* While my friend drove, I did a quick internet search and learned that this is a pregnancy in which the baby develops outside the uterus. Holy moly! What a nightmare! After what felt like the most painful sonogram in the history of womankind, I waited in the emergency room.

Finally, a sweet, very youthful Asian lady appeared, and she explained matter-of-factly: "Maria, you're having an ectopic pregnancy. Since the fetus may have ruptured in your fallopian tube, we need to bring you into surgery or you will die of internal bleeding."

My first thought? *Well, maybe I want to die, this world is such a mess!* Then I realized that dying would not fix anything, but forgiveness would.

After a complicated surgery and two blood transfusions, I regained consciousness in my recovery bed and started sobbing. I was sad, mad, hurt, and disillusioned. I felt so alone. Most of all, I felt like a victim. I was in a lot of pain, but soon I realized that I was really suffering more from the thoughts I was having. So I asked myself this pivotal question: *Why am I feeling this way?*

The answers came quickly: *I wish I hadn't slept with this*

guy. I wish I had not taken the Plan B pill. I wish I hadn't been so irresponsible....

What did all these thoughts have in common? They were all focused on what I had done in the past — the one thing I could not change! What I *could* change was how I viewed my predicament. I could see it in another way. I began to envision myself in a divine cocoon where I was taken care of, never alone, safe, and protected. That "cocoon" was the mind of God, where I could not be hurt.

All I could do about the past was to accept that I had done the best I could with the awareness I had. I was not bad, sinful, or guilty; I just hadn't known any better. Forgiving myself enabled me to stop regretting one thing after another and to become free of the past. I chose to remember only the love I gave and received — because that's what is real.

The miracle is that I stopped feeling as if I had lost something, and I began to feel that I had gained everything — because I learned that I could choose not to dwell in the past any longer.

Practice: Commitment Letter

Because we're often tempted toward unhappy ways of thinking, it's good to remember that forgiveness works best as a daily commitment. One way to remind yourself of your choice to forgive is to write a "commitment letter" to yourself. In this short letter, speak from your heart about what motivates you to follow through with your commitment.

As an example, here's the one I wrote for myself:

> My determination to forgive means that I constantly ask the Holy Spirit to help me see things another way, to be willing to change my perception. My commitment is to remember this world is not real, and that my home is in God, so I can laugh at the nonsense I have substituted for the love of God.
>
> I also commit to seeing with the vision of Christ, which means that I see no past or future. This way of seeing means I am the light of the world. I walk around in this dream shining the light of forgiveness, letting go of judgments and fears in order to bring true happiness to myself and others.

SUMMARY OF KEY POINTS

- Forgiveness removes the barriers to love, so that you can begin to see the world differently.
- Your judgments kill your happy!
- You cannot believe in love and fear at the same time.

- Forgiveness is a change of perception from fear to love.
- Any experience or feeling that is not coming from love is not real.
- You forgive people for what they did not do.
- You do the best you can with the awareness you have at the moment.

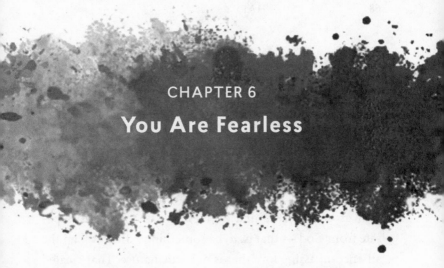

CHAPTER 6

You Are Fearless

I am not weak but strong. I am not helpless, but all-powerful. I am not limited but unlimited. I am not doubtful but certain. I am not an illusion, but a reality. I cannot see in the darkness, but in the light.

— *ACIM*, workbook lesson 91

Fear is the ego's way of holding our mind hostage. Some of my students are paralyzed by it; fear does not let them move on, find their purpose, or *live their happy*. I can hear how they've gotten stuck when they say things like:

"I have to stay overtime and be perfect at my job because if not, I am scared I will be fired."

"I can't write a blog. I am a writer, and it has to be perfect!"

"I can't stand up to my wife because then she will not let me see my child."

Most of us have believed the nonsense of this cuckoo voice for way too long. It has instilled in our unconscious the message "You don't deserve a happy ending," and I'm here to tell you nothing could be further from the truth. In this chapter I will help you understand that it is your divine right not only to have a happy ending but to awaken to the truth along the way. You must let go of the handcuffs of fear even if that feels very uncomfortable.

The Voice of Fear

Fear arose when we first decided it was possible to separate from God — that is, to be something different than the all-encompassing love that is our true nature. That created the opposite in our mind, and this is what we know as the *ego*, which is a god of fear. The ego continually makes us believe that situations "out there" are the source of our fear, and at times the ego even declares victory over these external events. But fear arises inside, and some fresh hell is always brewing in the mind, which accepts the conflicted thoughts of the ego. This dynamic explains the madness and violence of the human race's thoughts and actions in this collective dream we call life.

People are fearful because they have forgotten who they are. They're fearful because they have replaced their truth with dreams; they have fallen into a deep sleep and think the world is real. Now they don't know how to fix it and feel that they are trapped in darkness. The truth is that we still have light within us; we are just afraid to see it. What helps banish fear is the willingness to remember that we are in the mind of God.

To become fearless, we must know we possess a split mind: there is the ego, which is the voice of fear, and the

Holy Spirit, which is our bridge back to the love of God. Whenever we are not being ruled by the ego, we can be the "decision maker" who chooses between these parts of our mind.

What does that mean? I have learned that if I listen consistently for the voice of love within my mind, I don't experience fear. To do this, you have to decide to let go of judgments, regrets, and manipulations — that is, to let go of trying to make certain things happen. You have to decide to let go of worry and know that the Holy Spirit has your back.

That doesn't mean it's always easy to tell the difference between the voice of the ego and of the Holy Spirit. Here are some pointers for distinguishing these voices. Ego sounds like this:

- Ego makes you feel as if you have to take an action *right now* or else!
- Ego warns you about being harmed or losing something; it's reactive and defensive.
- Ego has high expectations for how things should turn out, and above all it wants to be right.
- Ego insists you must *do* something to find happiness — such as, to be happy, you must get the degree, get the parking space, get the guy or girl... blah blah, blah!

What the ego *doesn't* tell you is that the excitement of "getting" is temporary. Anything that is not of God could never fulfill you the way you truly want to be. No matter how many happy scenarios the ego convinces you to buy into, they will ultimately lead to an unhappy ending.

On the other hand, the Holy Spirit's voice is entirely different:

- The Holy Spirit makes you feel at ease; there is no rush because you will be told all you need to know and do.
- The Holy Spirit reminds you that there is nothing to lose or defend against.
- The Holy Spirit keeps you open and curious about what happens next.
- The Holy Spirit reminds you that "I need do nothing." It teaches you that everything is exactly perfect right now.

We can treat whatever seems to be a problem as a reminder to resist the ego's fearful advice in favor of the wiser voice within. Whether we face an IRS audit, a parking ticket, or bad news from the doctor, the Holy Spirit says, "Listen to me instead, and I will show you that only love is real." You'll know you've begun to listen when you feel enthusiastic and inspired!

Rafael: Learning to Hear a New Voice

Rafael had been fired from his job and was going through a divorce; his wife was giving him a hard time and making many demands on him if he wanted to continue being in his daughter's life. Every time they talked, it always turned into a fight, and then they stopped talking altogether. Rafael was living in Argentina, and his mother, a client of mine, convinced him to come to Los Angeles because she was worried about his drinking, pills, and depression. She asked me to give Rafael some spiritual counseling.

At our first meeting, Rafael looked riddled with fear as he walked through the door. He was obviously very sad, so we began by looking at how the ego was running wild in his mind. He was constantly overthinking, wishing he had done things differently in the past and worrying about the future. I asked him to consider the notion that the past was exactly perfect because he'd done what he thought was best at the time.

He also was thinking that he would never get along with his wife or have a relationship with his daughter. He couldn't sleep from worry about this dark future.

"That's what I call the ego's 'cuckoo' thinking," I gently suggested. "You can't sleep, and you're depressed about something that hasn't happened yet."

With help, Rafael became more aware of his delusional thinking, and he came to see that habitual fear and anxiety were not inevitable or beyond his power to change. In fact, he was actually choosing them by listening to the ego's crazy voice. Over several months, he began to sleep better and drink less, and he started meditating and journaling. In one of his meditations, he reported receiving the guidance in Spanish *No te preocupes* ("Don't worry"). Instead of fearing his wife, he got clear about his grievances and began to forgive them. He also became aware of judging his mom, and he learned to stop this by asking the Holy Spirit for help to see things differently.

In our last session, Rafael said he felt at peace. He planned to go back home to get his life in order, step by step. His problems weren't all solved, but he'd changed the way he was dealing with them, since he'd learned to take counsel from a different voice. It brought me such joy to see him with a big, fearless smile as he walked out my door the last time.

The only war worth fighting is in the mind. That's the source of all our conflicts, and that's the only place where we can resolve them. Once we have overcome the fear within our minds, there will be no more war outside.

Practice: Mantra for Reducing Fear

To help reduce fear, repeat the following mantra to yourself throughout the day: "I am the work of God, and his work is wholly lovable and wholly loving." Repeat this as often as you can. You can also use this for other people, especially those you have a grievance against. Say of them: "You are the work of God, and his work is wholly lovable and wholly loving." Practice this as a meditation with your eyes closed. Imagine yourself looking into a mirror and saying these words to yourself, or imagine people in front of you and say it to them.

The Power of Forgiveness

While resting on my couch after giving two services at Unity Burbank Center for Spiritual Awareness, I began to suffer over a man that I really liked. (Yes, this is a recurring grievance of mine.) Things weren't going the way I wanted; he wasn't texting me back or asking me out. As I thought of ways to text him and have him over for dinner — that is, as I considered how to manipulate the situation — I began feeling very anxious and insecure. This feeling was too familiar to me, and I became disappointed with myself. After all, I was a minister and spiritual leader now. I was supposed to have it together, not be falling apart after my services!

I was crying, having compulsive thoughts, and feeling very unworthy. So I asked the Holy Spirit if there was a way out. Could I be fearless and at ease and value myself in this moment — the very opposite of what I was feeling? This area of my life felt like a nightmare, and I was desperately ready for a makeover...*pronto*! Immediately I received this inspired thought:

You must forgive your father....Not only him but every man in your life.

Right away, I felt an unexpected peace come over me, and the tears stopped. But I was also confused. *Forgive my father?* He had died when I was three months old, and I had no memory of him. I couldn't see how our connection had hindered me in any way. I knew he had attempted suicide more than a dozen times before finally succeeding by shooting himself in the head. At the time, my mom was suffering. She'd already lost a son (one of my brothers, who died at age nine in a bicycle accident). My dad was also struggling with the pain of their son's death, and he also still felt guilty for leaving Cuba in 1966, when he left behind two other sons from a previous marriage.

I didn't remember my dad, but I was told that he was

so happy when I was born that the doctors thought he was no longer suicidal. Yet he killed himself three months later — and every time I thought about that I felt very sad. Now, I paid attention to that sadness, and instead of trying to forget it, I actually felt angry and nauseous. *He left me, and he left my mom. He left all of us alone to fend for ourselves!*

Then I made a connection: At the beginning of the relationship with my ex-husband, I often feared that he would leave me at any moment — just like my dad!

When I looked at this predicament with the Holy Spirit's help, this is the message I received:

> *What a joy that you are looking at this now with me. What appeared to happen to your dad has nothing to do with you, and there is nothing wrong with you. His life was his dream, his experience, and the lessons he chose. In truth your father never abandoned you because your true father within could not possibly leave you. You've been looking for men to replace the love that's always been within.*

After hearing this, I was moved to write a letter to my father:

Daddy,

I never got to tell you that I love you. I am sorry for all the pain you went through, and I trust you are in a better place. You are my prince, my guardian angel, because in truth I know you never left me and never will. We are one, you see. You are an amazing spirit who has been a great teacher. Your leaving your body was never about me, but somehow I decided to make it about me. I've carried this burden for so long. Whatever I have unconsciously made it mean till now is not true, and I am ready to let go of that cross. I am willing to forgive you, Dad.

After writing this letter, I received concise, specific, and practical instructions for a "Seven-Step, Seven-Day Fearless Practice." I had never seen or thought about a process like this before, and I knew I had to do it, even if it was out of my comfort zone and I was scared.

I describe this process below, and I followed it a full seven days, forgiving all the men in my life. It was one of the most emotional and painful things I have ever experienced, worse than my ectopic pregnancy. I had a speaking engagement that week, and I brought an assistant with me for support because I had hardly slept for days. I covered up the dark circles around my eyes with makeup, and I used what I was going through as a lesson in the talk, which went well.

Don't let this process of confronting your fears scare you. Think of it as something that will help bring back the memory of love to your mind.

Practice: Seven-Step, Seven-Day Fearless Practice

Here is the seven-step practice. In it, you focus on all the people who are directly related to a particular situation or problem. For instance, for me, I focused on my grievance with men, and I chose to include all my ex-boyfriends. The objective is to cover *everyone* involved in the situation by the end of seven days, so that you complete the process in a week. You tackle one person at a time, and you repeat steps 4 to 7 with each person. Also, have a computer or notebook handy so you can write down your thoughts at any point in the process. After seven days, my journal was fifteen pages long. Here are the steps:

1. Choose the problem that you most need to solve right now, the one that makes you significantly fearful, angry, or frustrated.

2. Go back in time and make a list of everyone involved in that problem. For example, if you identified insecurity as your problem, you might list people in your family, in school, and at work who have made you feel unworthy.

3. Over the course of seven days, bring to mind each person in order, starting with the person who goes farthest back into the past and continuing into the present. If your list includes more than seven people, you will have to do more than one person a day, and if you have less than seven, you would repeat some people.

4. Reflect on how one person made you feel and what you believe the person did to

you. Write out the story of how the person hurt you.

5. Open your mind to seeing the problem and person differently. Ask how you can find a way to feel powerful instead of frustrated or afraid. Write down the insights you get from the Holy Spirit.

6. Write the person a letter. As an example, see the letter I wrote to my dad (page 74).

7. Forgive the person using the chapter 5 practice "The Forgiveness Process" (page 61).

When I did this process, I was also guided to do the following along with it:

- I meditated at least ten minutes a day.
- I held loving thoughts in my mind throughout the day.
- In all situations, I asked: Is my choice or decision here aligned with my values?

You might find it helpful to do this process in the morning when you are fresh and rested. No matter how many people you include, continue the process for seven days, since that allows you to develop enough focus and intensity for things to really start changing. You might be surprised to see that the problem you begin with is not quite the same one you finish working on. Take your time and be gentle with yourself.

The deeper you go and the more honest you are, the more benefits you will receive. After I did the process, I felt as if I'd traveled from hell (feeling anxious, angry, and sad) to heaven (feeling peaceful, joyous, and happy). The problem I had begun with — trying to get a certain guy's attention and make him like me — wasn't "solved"; it just no longer mattered, once I decided to be fearless by healing my grievances with all the men in my life.

Through this practice, I was able to understand that my problem was never about men. So many of our problems are rooted in trying to find, force, or fantasize the love we already have within. What we need most of all is to stop fooling ourselves with these "problems." We can live happily ever after not by getting everything or everyone we want, but by finding the way to our own fearlessness within.

SUMMARY OF KEY POINTS

- Fear is the ego's way of holding our mind hostage.
- We become fearful when we forget who we are in spirit.
- We can learn to hear a new voice (the Holy Spirit) instead of the ego's voice of fear.
- Becoming fearless requires forgiving the past and opening our mind to a different way of seeing.
- The Seven-Step, Seven-Day Fearless Practice helps develop the focus and intensity to release the problems we think we have.

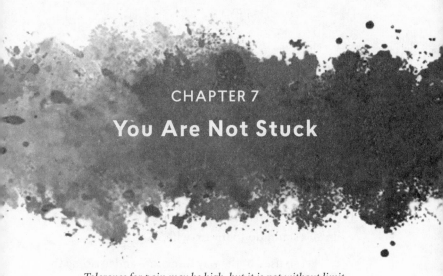

CHAPTER 7

You Are Not Stuck

Tolerance for pain may be high, but it is not without limit.
Eventually everyone begins to recognize, however dimly,
that there must be a better way. As this recognition becomes
more firmly established, it becomes a turning point.

— *ACIM*, chapter 2, section III

How are you doing? We have gone over quite a bit thus far. Some of it may speak to you and your issues, and some of it may not. Some parts you may understand better than others. That's okay. Just reading this far shows your willingness and your desire to change.

Hopefully, by now, you see that no matter how long you have been in pain, feeling sad, or thinking you've totally lost your happy, *this need not be* — there is another way. You really have to want it, though. The only way to real change is to think differently and to see beyond what you think you know.

I see this over and over again with my students and clients: They want to change, but not really. They'd like their lives to improve, but not at the cost of letting go of some *caca* thoughts and judgments. They say things like:

> "I would like to start my own company, but I don't
>   know how or where to start."
> "I would like to quit smoking, but I can't!"
> "I would like not to be a workaholic, but I have to
>   provide for my family."
> "I would like to spend more time with my kids, but
>   I can't stand up to my ex-wife."

We can get so used to the way things are and to doing the same thing every day that, even though we wish for change, we think we can't, so we don't even make an effort. We think we're stuck, without realizing it's merely our thoughts that are not going anywhere! But while our thoughts can keep us stuck, they can also get us going again. The Course explains (ch. 2, section VI):

> Few appreciate the real power of the mind, and no one remains fully aware of it all the time. However, if you hope to spare yourself from fear, there are some things you must realize, and realize fully. The mind is very powerful, and never loses its creative force. It never sleeps. Every instant it is creating. It is hard to recognize that thought and belief combine into a power surge that can literally move mountains. It appears at first glance that to believe such power about yourself is arrogant, but that is not the real reason you do not believe it. You prefer to believe that your thoughts cannot exert real influence

because you are actually afraid of them....There are no idle thoughts. All thinking produces form at some level.

How Our Thoughts Keep Us Stuck

We must pay close attention to our ego thoughts. We make them real by giving life to them and believing them — but that means we can change them. What holds us back from doing what we feel called to do is not "out there," but inside. What holds us back, or takes us forward, has to do with what we believe to be true at any given moment.

The way out of being stuck in the same old, same old is to understand that our experience comes from what we think, and we can give up what we are thinking. We do that by yielding our thoughts to our own higher mind, or Holy Spirit, so that we may see differently. This is what "choosing the miracle" means: choosing to see differently, and trusting that we have an intelligent power within — our own teacher of love — who will help us.

Pay special attention to the limiting or negative thoughts you don't want to give up. These are the kinds of thoughts you hang on to even though they don't make you feel good. Because what you see reflects your thoughts, the world appears hostile or frustrating whenever you are hooked on such *caca* thinking. Giving your thoughts over to the Holy Spirit helps you recognize that your real home is not in that crappy world, but *in the mind of God*. When you go home in your own mind, you will perceive Creation's true gentleness.

For illustration, here is how some specific limiting thoughts might be changed by giving them over:

- Thought: "I can't move from my hometown. It's all I know!"

  Holy Spirit: *I honor the calling in my heart to move. I am capable of moving anywhere.*

- Thought: "I would like to spend more time with my kids, but I am scared to ask my ex-wife. What if she takes me to court?"

  Holy Spirit: *I trust that all is falling into place even though it does not seem to be. I can get out of my own way and trust my inner wisdom. I have nothing to fear.*

- Thought: "I have to hang on to him. He is the love of my life!"

  Holy Spirit: *The love of my life is my true Self. I don't need anything or anyone outside myself to thrive. I am sustained by the love of God.*

Changing our thoughts in this way won't immediately solve our problems. But it will make it possible for them *to be released* because we will have access to the full creative power of our own inner wisdom. When we get stuck in a certain way of doing things, it's usually because we have excluded the best part of the mind — our spiritual intelligence — from awareness. That means we settle for those false beliefs that tell us things will stay the same forever, and this makes it pretty difficult to change the *now*. The weird thing is that we can get kind of comfortable with life being this way.

Comfort Zone = Unhappy Place

Our greatest happiness is to live a life fully expressed, and that's why getting out of our comfort zone will bring us good cheer. We think that our comfort zone is a nice place to be, but in fact it isn't. It's like getting used to sleeping on a folding chair because we haven't organized the room to put in a bed. Despite the discomfort, we may keep things that way because it's what we know. We are stuck, scared of the unknown.

Some of the most miraculous things happened when I moved to Los Angeles by stepping out of my first comfort zone, my hometown of Miami. I had dreamed of living in LA since I was a little girl. Every time I watched the popular 1980s sitcom *Punky Brewster*, I yearned to act in the show. Punky had an African American friend, and I really wanted to be her Latina friend! My mom told me the show was filmed in LA, and I knew that was far from Florida. My desire to live there strengthened through my teens and twenties, but I wouldn't dare move! I had lots of excuses: *It's too far from Miami. I'd miss my family. My acting career is blooming here. Miami is what I know.*

But one night after journaling, I had a vision of living in Miami forever, going to the same kinds of castings, and booking the same kinds of jobs. Eventually I'd do what women were supposed to: get married and get pregnant. Maybe that would be okay, but it would mean ignoring the calling in my heart since I was a child. I had to get unstuck and *move*! In my late twenties I left Miami to start again in Los Angeles.

Once there, I was led to becoming unstuck in a different way. As I described earlier, I joined the Course organization

Pathways of Light with the intention of healing my divorce. What I haven't shared is how fearful I was when I heard the calling to become a minister. I wanted to deny it. I remember saying to myself: *I am doing this to heal and to know more about the Course, not to be a minister. I am an actress!*

I resisted so much that it took me three years to finish a curriculum that only requires one. I also took six months off because I was still entranced by the world. It was very real for me. After a few months of self-destructive partying, drinking, and taking drugs, I was absolutely miserable, so tired of being stuck and unhappy. I registered for the next courses to get ordained, and I really began to listen to Spirit through the courses. I was ready! When Unity Burbank Center asked me to speak, I knew I had to step into my calling, and other unexpected opportunities to speak also showed up. I realized that, in LA, you can be an actress, TV host, *and* reverend!

I am beyond grateful that I finally started paying attention to the signs and said *yes* to my real work even though I was scared. I came back to my Pathways studies even though it was way out of my comfort zone. If I had not stepped into the *discomfort* zone, I would have remained self-destructive and not found my life purpose of helping people *live their happy*!

Compulsive Worry Keeps Us in Place

Do you have a problem that you think about all the time — as soon as you wake up and while brushing your teeth, driving to work, having lunch and dinner, and finally lying awake in bed when you should be sleeping? Rather than coming up with a solution, all you're doing is reviewing the same worries over and over: *How did I get into this fix? Why is this happening to me? Why won't this person do what I want? What if I do this or that? What if I say this or that?*

Compulsive worrying means believing that your problems are very real (what I call "big deals") and there really is no solution. You're depending on the wrong adviser in your own head; as the Course reminds us, "The ego's rule is, 'Seek and do not find.'" As long as you're listening to the ego's advice, you're going to worry about the same stuff over and over again. And worry is just another way of telling yourself, *This is the way it has to be. I need to worry. I need to suffer. I need to be unhappy.* If you believe in the nonsense of the ego, you end up being fooled!

To get unstuck from the same old problems, and to change your thoughts, it would be helpful to do these three things:

1.   You must recognize there is really only one problem: that you believe you separated from God (not true!) and should be punished for it.
2.   You must say *no mas* ("no more!") to compulsive worry.
3.   You must allow *happy* thoughts in the place of worried thoughts — even if you don't want to!

Changing your thoughts isn't a one-time deal; it's a *practice.* Understanding that you don't have to be stuck with the same old stuff is just the beginning. Then you have to start opening your mind to new thoughts and happier experiences. First, you must be mindful and present, staying aware of what you are thinking and feeling. When you find you're not at peace, notice that, and "choose again" in a way that makes sense to you. It can be as simple as thinking, "I choose to be happy now." Choose this again and again and again. With practice, happy thoughts will arise automatically whenever you feel stuck with a problem. That's when you'll start realizing that being unhappy always has more to do with how you think than with anything that happens to you.

Practice: Meditation for Getting Unstuck

I know you've heard that meditation eases stress and improves your general health. For me, the primary importance of meditation is that it helps amplify the loving voice of the Holy Spirit within. That's why I encourage my clients and students to do self-guided meditations. Before I share with you a specific and efficient meditation you can do on your own, let me share some tips that will make meditation easier:

- Go somewhere that is quiet, where you won't be disturbed.
- Breathe deeply, and return your attention to breathing whenever you can.
- If you can, light a candle and/or incense.
- Visualize what you are repeating to yourself. If you say in the silence, *I see a light on top of my head*, really bring that image to life in your mind.

To begin meditating, close your eyes and take a few deep breaths. Visualize a ball of golden light on the top of your head. Watch that light as it descends through your eyes, mouth, chest, and heart, where it may change color. The light continues all the way down to your toes. Breathe deeply again, and quietly say "peace" a few times.

Now, visualize an altar where you place all your worries and concerns. Perhaps you've wrapped them up in boxes of different colors, and maybe there are a lot of them. If the number of your worries makes you a little uncomfortable, wrap up your discomfort and place it on the altar as well.

Next, feel the presence of love next to your altar. Perhaps you see an image of an angel, saint, or Jesus; whatever symbol comes to you represents your personal connection.

Now, give everything you've placed on the altar to the symbol of love that you see. Declare the following: "God, I surrender all the worries, concerns, and negative beliefs that keep me stuck and unable to experience love. I choose you now instead. May your will be done."

When you feel finished, take a few more deep breaths and open your eyes.

These instructions are just a guide, a model that you can adapt for your own use. Whether or not you notice good effects after the first attempt, repeat this meditation every time you feel stuck, and it will deliver even better results. Don't be surprised if you find yourself changing the meditation each time. This is natural, and it indicates your increasing skill as a visualizer and meditator. The practice may also inspire other creative ways to surrender your "stuckness."

Don't worry if, during a meditation, you think about other things that don't seem pertinent. That's okay. It happens to me, especially if I'm hungry. I start to think of yummy Cuban dishes like black beans, white rice, and fried sweet bananas....¡Que rico!

When you recognize you're drifting, just bring yourself back and continue the meditation. Afterward, you can eat or do whatever you were thinking about!

Resilience

To live unstuck, you must grow your resilience. What is that? It means having the strength to move on, no matter the difficulties you're confronting. It's easy to fall into the trap of being stuck after a very trying and emotional event in your life. In an attempt to protect ourselves, we end up becoming victims of our circumstances, sometimes literally stopping our lives when faced with a traumatic crisis, like the loss of a job, divorce, or the death of a loved one.

My mom taught me what true resilience is.

In 1966, she left behind her homeland of Cuba because of the rise of Communism, and she could not take anything she owned beyond a single suitcase. With my dad and their two sons, she headed to Spain and then to New York before ending up in Miami — where in a terrible accident, my nine-year-old brother (whom I never met) was hit by a car and died. My mom was simultaneously mourning that loss and pregnant with me while trying to deal with a suicidal husband. Can you imagine how that felt? It must have been like hell on earth, especially because my dad did kill himself when I was three months old.

It is times like these when you can't afford to get stuck in hell. You must remember who and what you are, as best you can. Recalling your divinity will give you the strength to heal while you keep on with the demands of life. My mother couldn't afford to get stuck; she did not let the death of my father and my brother destroy her. She had the courage to pick herself up and step into her greatness. At that time it meant learning English, looking for a job, and caring for her family as best she could. My brother, then sixteen, got a job and helped with the expenses. In fact, he bought me my first crib, and later I have memories of him putting makeup on me at the cosmetics counter at the mall. My mother also remarried when I was four years old, providing me with an amazing father who has always seemed like my biological father. I have never called him a "stepdad." He told me that on the first date when he and my mom went to the beach (I came along since my mom could not get a babysitter), he saw me and thought: *This little girl will be my daughter. I will love her as if she were my own.* He sure has! He always allowed me to follow my dreams, even if he might have wished I had done things differently. He has always honored what I thought was best and supported me no matter what, as has my mom.

Resilience also teaches those around you. When I was in the hospital for my emergency surgery for the ectopic pregnancy, my brother flew from Miami to LA that same night and was at my bedside when I opened my eyes in the morning. He stayed with me at the hospital the whole time I was there, not even going home to shower. That is love and kindness. I think he could do that partly because he learned from our mother, who put our needs first and her struggles second. Her resilience gave me a happy childhood, as well as an amazing role model.

It's Not All about You

The "me, me, me" syndrome can also keep you stuck. To be self-centered means that you aren't being love-centered, since love is inclusive. *Amor es amor es amor es amor es amor.* . . . If you want to be free, you must have a we-are-all-one mentality, meaning you understand that there is plenty of love to go around, way more than enough for everyone, so it doesn't all have to center on you.

The Course suggests this liberating idea: "God is but love, and therefore so am I." It also suggests that we are *all* "teachers of God." That means *you* are a teacher of love. When you realize what this means, you don't have to worry about how much attention your "self" is getting because you know that your Self is the *source* of the very best attention there is. The more you give love, the more you have love!

That's not how the ego works, of course, because it teaches us that we never have enough attention, and so we must constantly seek more. That's never truly satisfying.

What is satisfying, and very deeply so, is to be a teacher of God, strutting in your truth, and busting out your happy game. Just like a dog sheds hair and the hair goes all over the place, you can be shedding light all over everyone and everything.

How do you do that? By doing the following:

- holding everything in high regard
- being grateful
- letting go of your "big deals"
- smiling a lot
- getting out of your own way and having spirit guide you

You will forget sometimes; it's easy to fall back into the frightened, selfish ego mode. But I promise that the more you catch yourself and choose love again, the easier it becomes, and the more you will gradually get yourself unstuck.

SUMMARY OF KEY POINTS

- We get stuck in life because of our thoughts, not our circumstances.
- Your "comfort zone" isn't really a happy place.
- You can release compulsive worrying through meditation (and you don't have to do it perfectly).
- Resilience is the strength to bounce back after misfortune — and we can teach it to each other.
- To find your happy, you have to let go of "me me me."

CHAPTER 8
You Are Getting Ready

Miracles arise from a miraculous state of mind,
or a state of miracle readiness.

— *ACIM*, chapter 1, Principle of Miracles 43

When athletes are getting ready for the Olympics, they train exceptionally hard and maintain a high level of commitment, drive, and practice. This is what needs to take place in you now! No more excuses, no more feeding your littleness. You have something to claim that is even better than a medal; you have your function to claim, which is the same as your happy. All that you have read in this book till now has been getting you ready for this. It's up to you! This book can't give this to you; you have to really want it. That's what I had to do, and that meant getting out of my own way so that I was no longer contradicting what I yearned for.

Here is some of the limiting self-talk I had to change so I could get ready:

"I know that I am love itself, but I still want to look
    for a man to make me happy."

"I believe that I have inner abundance, but I don't
    have enough money in the bank."

"I am a great actress, but auditions scare the hell
    out of me!"

In the introduction, I shared about my struggle with going to church, reading self-help books, including the Course, and remaining unhappy. I had some good ideas, but I was out of sync with my true Self. I wanted to live a happy life, but my thoughts and actions were not aligned. I was stuck in littleness, while at the same time wanting to live my magnitude. When we hang on to our separate selves with separate interests, we lose awareness of our true Self because Oneness and individuality cannot coexist.

What Is Littleness?

Littleness is the self you have identified with since you thought you separated from God — that is, the constant awareness of love. It's the part of your mind that feels limited and unworthy. Most of us usually function from this tiny space and don't even know it! Defending your individuality means you are preserving littleness. When you search for your happiness as a gift you want from the world, you are actually protecting your separateness. The Course puts it this way: "When you strive for anything in this world in the belief that it will bring you peace, you are belittling yourself and blinding yourself to glory" (*ACIM*, ch. 15, section III).

We seek and try to pile up all the little fragmentations

of the world as a substitute for having *everything*. We get caught in thinking that these pieces of the whole will eventually give us our happy. This is why the topic of "abundance" is popular. We're encouraged to imagine getting the perfect relationship, the great car, the successful career, and all that, unaware that we are actually feeding our littleness. We wish for things like more money because we feel little and deprived. The solution is not to get more of anything, but to recognize the abundance within. Before I describe True Abundance, let's get perfectly clear about its opposite.

False Abundance

Living in this world, we are tempted to define abundance in material terms. We're endlessly working to get enough things and money, sometimes succeeding and sometimes not so much. The endless search for "more" is one of the ego's favorite ways to entrance you, yelling: "You can only get your specialness from what you own and wear and from impressing people!"

¡Pero eso es pura mierda! "What a bunch of *caca*!" Oh, you might get a nice suit to wear when you accept an award you've won and feel happy for a hot second. But that kind of happy doesn't last; it's a trick. When you really take a look at what I like to call "the Ego's BS-Abundance System," you will see that it's rooted in a sense of lack that never goes away. A month later, the award or the nice suit won't mean very much, and you'll be on the hunt for something new and satisfying. How can that be abundance?

You simply can't *live your happy* if you think that your

abundance is outside you and that it has to be frequently replenished from external sources. Never! So let's look at the kind of abundance that helps you let go of littleness, instead of reinforcing it.

What Is True Abundance?

The constant awareness of *amor* in your mind, knowing that it is your natural inheritance, is the abundance that's rightfully yours. It's when you know that you are one with All, that you are holy and whole. Nothing outside defines you because you know you have it all right now.

This very moment, close your eyes and just be. Try not to think of anything. See yourself melting into your bed or chair. Feel the air around you. Now open your eyes and take a breath. Settle into stillness, and you will get a glimpse of what is real.

True abundance is recognizing that *you are as God created you*. That means you feel no lack within you, so that you don't have to roam the world endlessly, trying to get your fix.

You may ask: *How can I believe in this type of abundance? I need a roof over my head, money, and clothes!*

I get that! Living in this world, it does appear that we need things. But when you can always find your stillness, you'll always have an inner companion to help you find what you truly need for practical purposes. You won't have to give up clothing (that would be interesting) or eating. But you will know that *the things of this world are not what you are*. Because you can always find your own inner wealth, you will know that you're so much more than whatever petty trinkets could give you.

I am not saying you can't enjoy yourself or the stuff of this world; just watch what you are doing! Don't get lost in it all. Don't let it define you. Living in true abundance, you may attract the finer things of life — but you'll actually enjoy them more when you don't have to fear losing them. You are conscious now, experiencing abundance you can't put a price on.

Realizing My Abundance

Being an actress and TV host for all my adult life, I never had a steady income. I only made money when I booked a job. This helped me build trust in the flow of income in my life and the confidence to know that I am always provided for. There were times after my divorce when I found my- self down to my last thousand dollars, and I never worried about it. I paid my bills gladly, knowing that my source is plentiful. I have never really suffered from scarcity thinking, and thank goodness! (My grievances with men have been enough of a learning challenge.)

In the spring of 2013, I decided to move from my place in Los Angeles at a time when the real-estate market was in shambles. The only good option for me was to short-sell my condo. One day I was taken aback when the very nice guy handling my short sale said to me, as if he were asking a question: "*You are so happy?* You went through a divorce, you had a miscarriage, you have no money, you're going through a short sale, and you are *happy*? How?"

At that moment I had a rush of love run through my body because I realized how free I felt. I was grateful and proud of myself, and I hadn't really noticed before. It was a beautiful moment. I said, "Yeah, I'm happy. I know that none of this stuff really matters. I am eternally provided for, and it has nothing to do with this world." Suddenly, I could see all the things that had happened to me as gifts, each one an opportunity to remember my wholeness again. This is true abundance, and I'm grateful I was finally ready for it!

Practice: An Abundance Prayer

Here is a brief prayer that you can use as written, or adapt in your own words, to help you focus your intention on finding your true abundance within. If you're struggling with money or other material shortcomings, use it daily to get to the source of the problem.

Thank you, God, for the awareness of abundance in my mind. I am willing to understand my inheritance at a deeper level. I let go of my identification with my body and all external things. I step into your arms and recognize that I have everything and lack nothing. Standing in truth, I am one with all, whole and holy. Thank you, God, for never abandoning me, for always being here within. And thank you for giving me the Holy Spirit as a divine tool for realizing awareness, which never really leaves.

The Happy NOW!

To be ready for happiness, you must be in the present moment, as focused as Olympic athletes who put all their energy into what they are about to do. While you can merely *exist* without much awareness of where you are or what you're doing, *being is presence*. When you are present, you are not regretting or missing the past or anticipating the future. In the happy present, you hear the Holy Spirit's guidance and can actually experience eternity within a "holy instant." Just that instant is sufficient to "re-establish perfect sanity, perfect peace, and perfect love," suggests the Course.

Right now is it! It's your point of power, when you can choose to be the happiest being possible. *Right now* is when you can choose again, no matter what happened five minutes ago. *Right this second*, as you read this, you have the power to change your experience by changing your thoughts. But you can't do that *right now* if you are worrying about the past or the future. All you need to do is be present and see what happens. You will be guided on where to go, what to do, what to say, and to whom. "When you learn to decide with God, all decisions become as easy and as right as breathing. There is no effort, and you will be led as gently as if you were being carried down a quiet path in summer" (*ACIM*, ch. 14, section IV).

One of my favorite tools I use to keep me in the Happy

Now is the mantra: "I need do nothing." You're probably thinking: *What do you mean? Of course I need to do things. I need to pay my bills, I need to go to the bank, I need to brush my teeth....*In truth, you don't need to. You *want to* or *choose to*. For example, you don't need to pay your bills. You want to pay your bills because you know there will be certain consequences you *don't want* if you don't pay them.

You're making a choice of your own volition; you're not being pushed around by forces more powerful than yourself. You're dealing with the everyday world in the ways you've chosen. This way of thinking helps you keep your sense of power and responsibility. Beyond that, the only thing you *need* to do is to let the highest, wisest part of your mind, the Holy Spirit, guide your decisions. Then everything falls into place in ease and grace. You don't have to plan against the worst possible outcomes. Instead you can allow the best to happen.

Practice: Practicing Presence

When you get up in the morning, be present to your every move: Put your feet on the floor and notice how that feels. As you grab the toothbrush, be present and think, *Hey, look what I can do!* Maybe that sounds silly, but it really helps to acknowledge that you are *choosing* to brush your teeth at that moment, and you're pretty good at it! Do this when you open the refrigerator or brush your hair (*Wow,*

I'm really great at this! Practice helps!). Whatever you do, fully appreciate that you've chosen it.

Most of us experience plenty of opportunities to be present while driving. When you're at a red light, instead of thinking about where you are going, or that you're late or hungry, be present to your surroundings. What's around you? Drop any thoughts of the past or future, and try this thought: *This moment is just perfect!* Perhaps you can look over to the person in the car next to you, or someone on the street, and send them blessings in your mind. Wish them the best.

Finally, appreciate your moment in traffic by thinking: *Wow, I am the creator of this! I put myself here to see all this energy doing its thing at this exact time.* Be thankful for the gift of being.

With practice, you can apply this skill of presence to every situation you find yourself in. Even if the circumstance or event seems mundane at first, your presence can make it extraordinary. This will help you jump on the *happy train....*

Choo! Choo!

Get Ready to Live Your Happy

To get ready to *live your happy*, ask yourself these questions, as honestly as possible:

- What am I making real that's hurtful to myself or others?

- What am I making special? How do I make myself special?
- How am I playing out the separation in my life?
- How am I addicted to my littleness?

You can't *live your happy* with any exceptions. You're all in or you're not. You have to want it. You need to say the following with conviction and mean it:

- I am ready to let go of my grievances.
- I am ready to stop looking for happiness outside myself.
- I am ready to forgive.
- I am ready to stop judging.
- I am ready to feel worthy.
- I am ready to see things differently.
- I am ready to release all illusions.
- I am ready to live in the mind of God.

And you'd *better* be ready — because in chapter 9 we are coming home!

SUMMARY OF KEY POINTS

- Littleness is the self you have identified with since you thought you separated from God — that is, the constant awareness of love.
- We seek all the little fragmentations of the world as a substitute for having everything.
- You simply can't *live your happy* if you think that your abundance is outside yourself and that it has to be frequently replenished from external sources.

- True abundance is recognizing that *you are as God created you.*
- When you are present, you are not regretting or missing the past or anticipating the future.
- Presence means accepting that you have chosen to do what you want, instead of feeling forced by what you "need" to do.
- You can practice presence at any moment, under any circumstances.

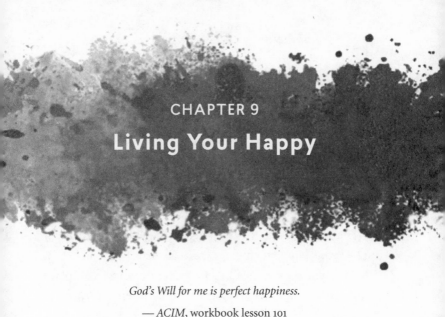

CHAPTER 9

Living Your Happy

God's Will for me is perfect happiness.

— *ACIM*, workbook lesson 101

¡*Felicidades!* Congratulations! You have made it to the *happy* ending! I can assure you that after reading this you will never experience this world the same. You have now put on Holy Spirit glasses, and you are not only looking super cool but also seeing things differently. For this you can be grateful. You have come this far with BIG willingness.

Right this moment, acknowledge yourself for diving into this book and for your commitment to *living your happy*.

You can also acknowledge what you could have done better. Everything you've attempted has brought you to where you are now, in this perfect moment. From now on, you will no longer tolerate your littleness. No more games, no more *caca*. You are now committed to live as God created you. You can fully declare:

> I am loving, and *I AM love*.
> I am peaceful, and *I AM peace*.
> I am abundant, and *I AM abundance*.
> I am happy, and *I AM happiness*.
> I am trusting, and *I AM trust*.

The last statement brings us to the last ingredient of the *live your happy* recipe: *trust*. To awaken to the love that is your true Self, you need to be aware of where you place your trust. I would like to distinguish between *old trust* and *new trust*.

Old Trust versus New Trust

Old trust is the kind you learned growing up. It is the faith you place in your limited perceptions, such as: *I am going to trust you because you seem like a good person. I am going to trust this situation because in the past it worked out*, and so on. The old trust relies on your little self. The old trust presumes you are separate from the world: You unconsciously believe that projecting your fears out into the world will liberate you from them, and you expect external things to make you happy.

All this is the ego's style of trusting.

New trust is the kind that will set you free from all your supposed problems. With new trust, you believe in love as your very essence, which means you identify with a different Self. There is no worry regardless of what's happening around you because you place your trust in love to heal all your misperceptions. This trust brings you peace, love, and much joy! New trust relies on the Holy Spirit. As the Course says: "You have very little trust in me as yet, but it will increase as you turn more often to me instead of to your ego for guidance. The results will convince you increasingly that this choice is the only sane one you can make. No one who learns from experience that one choice brings peace and joy while another brings chaos and disaster needs additional convincing" (*ACIM*, ch. 4, section VI).

I began grasping the concept of new trust when I was collaborating with mystic David Hoffmeister, my dear friend and colleague. We were going to give a talk together at Unity Burbank Center entitled "Night of Miracles." This was one of my very first collaborations, and I was quite excited and nervous! I remember getting to the church and asking David, "Hey, so what are we going to talk about?"

He said, "I don't know."

I was stunned! I asked, "What do you mean?"

"Let's just show up and let spirit guide us," he calmly suggested. I was like...*Oh, okay*. Even though I was a bit nervous, that felt right. And our two-hour talk was exceptional, as we both allowed spirit to move through us. David's calm and trusting presence gave me the confidence to step back and allow.

After that experience, my idea of trust changed. I began to unhook myself from the "problems" of this world. I allowed everything to happen without worry or judgment, which meant getting "me" out of the way.

New Trust Changed My Life

Another time, after flying home from giving a talk in Colorado, I was unpacking and thinking of what I would make for dinner. I had visions of an eggplant pasta dish with a glass of exquisite pinot noir. But the vision was interrupted when I could not find my video camera! Realizing that I'd left it under the seat of the plane, I felt a flash of fear. I used that camera to record all my talks and help get my message out; now I would have to buy a new one! I considered driving all the way back to the airport to hunt down the camera, but I hesitated, since that would mean I'd miss out on the great dinner I'd been planning. What if going to the airport was all for nothing? I felt myself sinking into a whirlpool of victimized feelings that were all too familiar.

Then, in a blink of an eye, my fear vanished as I realized, *If I am supposed to get the camera back, I will.* I trusted that it would all work out, rather than fearing the worst and feeling sad about one outcome or the other. At that moment, all uncertainty about what to do faded. I quickly grabbed a protein bar and headed out the door! By the time I reached the airport, it was 10 PM, and all the baggage offices were closed except for the airline I needed (Spirit Airlines, of course). The one attendant available was on the phone, and another passenger came in at the same time I did, but I let him get in line first because I got the message: *When you trust, there is never any rush.* I felt so calm I hardly recognized myself.

When I finally got the attendant's attention and told her I'd left a bag under the seat on my plane, she took down my information and said, "It could have been stolen."

Without knowing why, I answered, "No, that's not possible."

She shrugged and spoke into her walkie-talkie, trying to find someone working at the gate. There was no response, so she said, "I'll call you later if we find it. It could be a while."

But trust told me to be patient and firm. "I'm in no rush. I'll wait until someone answers."

To my surprise, she smiled and responded, "Let's go to the gate!" She shut off the lights, closed the door, and we headed upstairs. When she headed for the restricted area, she asked me to wait in a hallway. After twenty minutes she reappeared and said she couldn't find anyone, so I should leave and she'd call me later. But I still knew I should wait, and she was nice enough to try again. In a few minutes, she returned with my camera bag over her shoulder, asking, "Is this it?"

As I drove away from the airport that night, I cried tears of joy — not because I got my camera back, but because I had done things so differently than I used to. I didn't stay home feeling victimized by fate or blaming myself for losing my camera. When we truly trust, we don't just give in and wait for good things to happen. We actually find ourselves being more energetic and assertive than we would be in a state of distrust. After that episode, I was never the same. I no longer worry.

Dive into Trust

You have to dive into full trust if you want to *live your happy*. You have to get out of your own way and allow the

Holy Spirit to guide you. When the ego's dream is no longer real for you, you begin to have fun! Ever since you forgot that you are love, you have trusted the voice of doubt, fear, and worry. That was okay when you didn't know any better; now that you have read this book, there is no excuse. Now you do know better!

If you forget, here's a quick, four-step guide to getting back on track with trust. I wish I'd had such a guide back in the day when I was suffering unnecessarily. Thank God, I have it now — and so do you!

1. Whatever shows up, observe, be aware, and admit it. If you feel scared, let it be. Don't resist! Instead of letting fear run away with you, use this feeling to come back to truth. Don't judge any feelings you have; they are just feelings, and they'll pass sooner or later. The question is how you use them.

2. Ask yourself: *What am I making into a big deal?* For example, perhaps you got a ticket or a bad grade; perhaps your spouse cheated or a loved one died. We're all quick to judge such events fearfully, but believe it or not, we have another choice. You can let go of your old way of judging and allow judgment to be handled by your true Self. You can simply say: *Holy Spirit, judge this for me.*

3. Then, get out of the way. Even when you experience judgments, justifications, guilt, and fear, you can get out of your own way by turning them over to your "higher power." That's how they become signals for getting back to the truth.

4. Finally, trust. The three previous steps bring you to this power. When you trust in your higher Self, you know that all is unfolding perfectly. Even when you habitually or regularly forget, this step will remind you that you are as God created you.

Here's an image to help you remember this process: Imagine holding a bow and arrow and aiming for the Truth. First, you pull the arrow in. This means taking responsibility for everything you feel, no matter how sharp or dangerous it may seem. Maybe you've been poking yourself with this arrow for a long time and watching yourself bleed; that doesn't matter now. By agreeing to trust, you have picked up the bow of Spirit, which helps you aim that arrow in the right direction. Bring the arrow in, close to your heart, knowing that it's all yours. Pull in knowing that you are capable, you are unlimited, you are in a state of grace, and nothing can take that away from you. Then let the arrow go and... *trust*. When you hit the target of Truth, you'll know because of the *happy* feeling you get. If you don't hit the target, you probably still have plenty of arrows to work with....

Practice: The Happy Plan

The mind needs spiritual practice and discipline. As we learn consistent self-awareness and become free of conflict within our own thoughts, we can then wake up to our real purpose. As *A Course in Miracles* puts it: "My function and my happiness are one." That's what I mean by *living your happy*, and it's not just for your sake, but for everyone. I've found it helpful to focus my awareness and intention by following what I call a Happy Plan, which can be followed for two months at a time. The plan has five steps:

1. Set intentions.
2. Write and repeat affirmations.
3. Make commitments.
4. Stay open and willing.
5. Write prayers.

As an example, below is one of the Happy Plans I completed, which you can adapt to your own circumstances. Even if your plan changes along the way, it's very helpful to have a plan to refer to on a daily basis, reminding you of what you mean to be doing. Otherwise, a forgetful way of living can easily overtake you!

Happy Plan for May and June

1. Intention: Peace
2. Affirmations:

    I am the peace of God.
    I choose the peace of God now.
    I allow the Holy Spirit to be in charge of
        my mind.

3. Commitments:

    Declare affirmations every day.
    Be mindful and ask the Holy Spirit for help.

Read prayer morning and night.
Work out five days a week.
Meditate every day, no less than ten minutes.

4. I am willing and open to:

Visit my family in Miami.
Produce "One Love" inspirational concert.
Create new website.
Speak abroad.

5. Prayer:

"The end is certain, and the means as well.
To this we say 'Amen.' You will be told exactly what God wills for you each time
there is a choice to make.... And so we walk
with Him from this time on, and turn to
Him for guidance and for peace and sure
direction. Joy attends our way. For we go
homeward to an open door which God has
held unclosed to welcome us" (from *ACIM*,
workbook epilogue).

Now Get Excited!

Living your happy means being grateful both for what is
working and for what is *not* working in your life. You can
do this because your happiness is not dependent on what's
happening "out there." Your happiness reflects the growth
of your own inner awareness, compassion, and contact with
inner wisdom. Your happiness doesn't come from the world;
happiness is what you are. It exists within you! It always has

and always will, throughout all eternity. I'm reminded of this when I get home every day because my dogs, Sasha and Sophie, are always excited and happy to see me, no matter what might have happened that day. They always have the same excitement about what they love, and that's a way of life that's good for anyone.

Now that you know how your mind works and that you have the power to choose your experience, you can get excited about no longer having to suffer. Get excited that now you know you're not bad, you're not going to hell, you're not alone, you know what true forgiveness is…and get excited that all this means you are finally ready to get out of your own way and *live your happy*!

Acknowledgments

First, I would like to acknowledge myself for getting out of my own way and writing this book after suffering from dyslexia, having insecurities about grammar, and never, ever believing I would write a book! So here's to the "pinot noir" post on Facebook that led to all this happening.

Heartfelt thanks go to: my dear parents, Maria Sosa and Pablo Sosa; my brother, Jesus Felipe; Revs. Robert and Mary Stoelting at Pathways of Light (POL) for the amazing teachings that inspired the contents of this book; my POL facilitator, Rev. Johannys Jimenez-Hartog, for inspiring me to become a minister; Tom Vargas for making sure my message got out there; everyone at Unity of Burbank for giving me my first opportunity to speak and supporting me since day one; my dear colleagues David Hoffmeister and Gary Renard for supporting me and encouraging me; Georgia Hughes for believing in the book and saying YES to publishing it; my students and clients for being willing to be happy; and my agent and editor, D. Patrick Miller, for convincing me to write this book and taking this happy ride with me. Patrick, I could not have completed this book without you. Last, to the Holy Spirit for having my back and guiding me along the way.

About the Author

A Cuban American born in Miami, Maria Felipe is a dynamic international speaker, teacher, and minister. She leads monthly services in both English and Spanish at the Unity Burbank Center for Spiritual Awareness in Burbank, California. Prior to settling in California, Maria pursued a modeling and acting career. She appeared in national commercials and hosted successful TV shows, including World Wrestling Entertainment shows with live audiences of twenty thousand. After experiencing an inward calling, she changed course and studied with Pathways of Light, an accredited religious school inspired by *A Course in Miracles*.

Her talks draw both Spanish and English speakers from all over Southern California. She has appeared as a motivational speaker on television shows and news programs for

Univision, Telemundo, and CNN en Español. *People* magazine once referred to Maria Felipe as *una campeona sin rival*, or "a champion without rival."

Connect with Maria at:
www.mariafelipe.org
www.facebook.com/mariafelipefanpage
www.youtube.com/MariaCoconutTV
and on Twitter @revmariafelipe